THEMES IN
MACROECONO
HISTORY

THE UK ECONOMY, 1919–1939

THEMES IN MACROECONOMIC HISTORY

THE UK ECONOMY, 1919–1939

Solomos Solomou
Faculty of Economics, Cambridge

CAMBRIDGE
UNIVERSITY PRESS

Published by the Press Syndicate of the University of Cambridge
The Pitt Building, Trumpington Street, Cambridge CB2 1RP
40 West 20th Street, New York, NY 10011–4211, USA
10 Stamford Road, Oakleigh, Melbourne 3166, Australia

First published 1996

Printed in Great Britain at the University Press, Cambridge

A catalogue record for this book is available from the British Library

Library of Congress cataloguing in publication data

Solomou, Solomos.
Themes in macroeconomic history: the UK economy, 1919–1939
Solomos Solomou.
p. cm.
Includes bibliographical references.
ISBN 0 521 43033 X (hc). – ISBN 0 521 43621 4 (pbk.)
1. Great Britain – Economic conditions – 1918–1945.
2. Great Britain – Economic policy – 1918–1945. I. Title.
HC256.3.S56 1996
330.941083 – dc20   95-35069
CIP

ISBN 0 521 43033 X hardback
ISBN 0 521 43621 4 paperback

To Alexi and Chloë

CONTENTS

ACKNOWLEDGEMENTS

In writing this book I have received valuable comments and advice from Steve Broadberry, Roderick Floud, Tim Hatton, Michael Kitson, Patrick McCartan and the anonymous publisher's referees. The book has its origins in lectures I have given at Cambridge University and Stanford University: many thanks to all the students who have listened. Many of the research findings reported in the book have resulted from research projects funded by the ESRC (grants R000231387 and R000231814).

Thanks are due to Patrick McCartan, as economics editor of the Press, and Anne Rix, copyeditor of the Press, for handling the book efficiently. A special thanks to Alexi and Chloë for elongating the gestation of the book and to Wendy for creating the idea for the project.

NOTE ON THE TEXT

Throughout the text asterisks refer to entries in the
Glossary on pages 166 to 178.

CHAPTER 1

EPOCHS IN ECONOMIC HISTORY, 1919–39

INTRODUCTION

The interwar era has been embedded in the collective memory of policy-makers and economists as an epoch of mass unemployment, poor long-run economic growth, disintegrating world trade and excessive volatility in real output. These descriptive details imply that the period was one of change relative to the past. Change, however, does not *necessarily* mean discontinuity with the past. This chapter evaluates a number of perspectives on the phasing of economic growth as a way of gaining an insight into the extent of continuity and change over time. In order to help the student appreciate the kind of changes that were taking place in the interwar era the appendix to this chapter provides a pictorial survey of some of the key variables that are of interest to macroeconomists.

ECONOMIC EPOCHS AS LONG CYCLES

Economic growth in modern industrial societies has sometimes been viewed in terms of long cycles in output and prices with an approximate duration of fifty to sixty years, often referred to as Kondratieff waves.[1] The cycle is described by a series of

---

[1] Named after the Russian economist N.D. Kondratieff who analysed the price and output movements of the major industrial countries for the period 1780–1920.

alternating fast and slow phases of economic growth. Kondratieff and a number of more recent empirical analyses (Van Duijn, 1983; Kleinknecht, 1987) offer the following historical timing for the phases of the long cycle:

1850–73	Fast economic growth
1873–96	Slow economic growth
1896–1920	Fast economic growth
1920–39	Slow economic growth

Within this framework the interwar period is viewed as the downswing phase of a long cycle, encapsulating an era of slow economic growth, poor investment opportunities, mass unemployment and price deflation. At first sight this approach to history seems a promising one: the phases of economic growth depicted above are also episodes we find discussed in the economic history of the UK, such as the 'Great Victorian Boom' (1850–73), the 'Great Depression' (1873–96), and the 'Belle-epoque Boom' (1896–1913). However, the empirical evidence that has been accumulated over recent years suggests that this interpretation of long-run trends is unable to provide an empirically valid phasing of UK economic growth. The long cycle literature has tended to focus on price and monetary movements, neglecting the evidence for the 'real' side of the economy. With better and more extensive data on aggregate production and investment than were available in Kondratieff's time we have to reevaluate his description of trends in the UK economy: aggregate output and productivity growth fail to display the long cycle that Kondratieff assumed (Matthews *et al.*, 1982; Solomou, 1987). The discontinuities of economic growth observed in the interwar period need to be conceptualised within a more historical approach.

MADDISONIAN EPOCHS

A useful approach that places the interwar period in a long-run historical perspective, but not in a cyclical framework, is

Maddison's theory of epochs in capitalist development. Maddison (1982, 1991) rejects the long cycle framework as being an ahistorical model of economic change; instead he argues that economic growth has followed a number of *episodic* epochs resulting from institutional and policy regime changes that are specific to each period. The epoch of the classical gold standard* (c.1870–1913) represents a successful phase of economic growth while the period 1913–50 is one of slow and highly volatile economic growth. Each economic epoch is characterised by a number of 'system characteristics', defined by:

- the government's approach to demand management
- the bargaining power and expectations of labour
- the degree of freedom of trade and factor movements
- the character of the international payments system

The interwar period witnessed adverse shifts in a number of these system characteristics: the effect of the First World War on the labour market accelerated the unionisation of the labour force; protection in trade increased in the early 1920s and again in the 1930s; immigration laws in the New World during the 1920s regulated and restricted international labour movements; the classical gold standard of the pre-1913 era gave way to flexible exchange rates in the early 1920s, maladjusted fixed exchange rates in the mid 1920s and discretionary managed rates in the 1930s. Maddison's approach suggests that the national and international institutional features of the interwar period were unable to sustain the rates of economic performance achieved during the period 1870–1913. His approach has similarities with the 'maladjustment school' interpretation of interwar problems, as expressed by the majority report of the Financial Committee of the League of Nations (1932), set up to explain the world depression of 1929–32. This committee argued that deep-seated maladjustments and distortions, partly caused by the First World War,

3

were largely responsible for the problems of depression and unemployment during the interwar period.

A great deal of emphasis in recent research has been devoted to the impact of the transition to a gold exchange standard in the interwar period. The large exchange rate movements of the early 1920s prevented a more stable reconstruction period of the world economy after the First World War, and the gold standard rules that operated into the early 1930s generated an exceptionally severe world depression as countries had to deflate to sustain the credibility of the gold standard (Temin, 1989; Eichengreen, 1992; Bernanke and James, 1991). Thus, in order to achieve a smoother adjustment after the First World War a different set of institutional arrangements for the world economy were needed. These institutional developments were not to be seen until the New International Economic Order established under the Bretton Woods* international payments system after the Second World War.

Maddison's perspective offers some very useful insights into the role of institutions and institutional change in generating variations in economic growth. The inability of the major countries in the world economy to set up a more appropriate response to the shocks of the First World War is at the heart of explaining the key problems of the interwar era. We should, however, tread carefully if we are to prevent this analysis from becoming a circular perspective along the following lines of argument: *appropriate institutions are important to sustaining economic growth; the interwar era was an epoch of unemployment and slow economic growth; therefore, institutions failed in the interwar period.* There are a number of important propositions in this black box that need to be analysed further. Although we can make a convincing case that the attempt to return to the gold standard hindered UK economic performance during the 1920s, a case has to be made that the return to gold operated as a long-run constraint over the whole of the interwar period.

This idea is considered further when we evaluate the effects of the macroeconomic policy regime of the 1920s (chapter 2). Many of the other system characteristics also need to be considered in a critical perspective. The increased bargaining power of labour has often been held responsible for the mass unemployment and the higher output volatility of the era. This is a view expounded by some contemporary economists (such as Pigou, 1927) and more recently by some economic historians (Benjamin and Kochin, 1979). The causal paths by which this comes about are not always convincing, as is shown in chapter 3.

In Maddison's framework major institutional and policy regime shifts can make the system characteristics unfavourable to sustaining rapid economic growth. A more general hypothesis that has been emphasised in the recent macroeconomics literature is the theory of 'random walks'*: this perspective argues that many different type of shocks can move the economy from one path to another. Thus, economies do not have a natural tendency to settle on a unique path determined by long-run supply-side conditions; instead the economy moves along paths determined by the nature of specific historical shocks. The important point of departure of the random walk idea is that both *transitory* and *permanent* shocks can have a displacing effect on the equilibrium path of an economy. History matters, in the sense that transitory events can leave the economy in a permanently changed state. For example, the overvaluation of the UK real exchange rate during 1920–2 (Broadberry, 1986) may have had persistent adverse effects, despite an improvement in the competitiveness of the exchange rate after 1922 (see chapter 2). This approach emphasises a high degree of discontinuity in the path of the economy, justifying an analysis of the kind of shocks and institutional changes that are specific to the interwar experience.

INTERWAR ECONOMIC PERFORMANCE IN A LONG-RUN PERSPECTIVE

In the light of this survey let us consider the long-run macroeconomic performance of the UK. While a long-run approach to economic growth has the advantage of giving us more information about the dynamics of the growth process, the further back we move in historical time the less reliable is the macroeconomic data that we need to consider. For example, the three estimates of GDP before 1913 (income, expenditure and output) have large measurement errors that make it very difficult to determine the time path of the macroeconomy (Solomou and Weale, 1991). However, while these errors are very important to our perception of short-run economic behaviour (such as business cycles), they do not affect our perception of the long-run growth process. All the three estimates of GDP show that aggregate real output was growing at approximately 2 per cent per annum between 1870 and 1913 (Feinstein et al., 1982; Solomou, 1987; Crafts et al., 1989). Deviations about this mean growth rate did take place but the macroeconomy showed a tendency to return to the underlying long-run growth rate. This pattern of growth can be described as 'trend-stationary'* and is illustrated in a stylised form in figure 1.1.

Describing the initial growth conditions of the pre-1913 period as 'trend-stationary' along a steady path is quite different from the idea that UK macroeconomic performance underwent a 'climacteric' at the end of the nineteenth century: this latter perspective depicts the UK economy as undergoing a deceleration in trend growth during 1870–1913 and particularly during the Edwardian period, 1899–1913 (Feinstein et al., 1982). The evidence for this view comes from an analysis of the compromise estimate of GDP (an average of the income, expenditure and output estimates) which shows growth rates

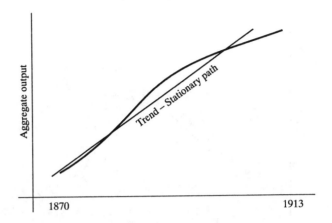

Figure 1.1: A stylised view of pre-1913 economic growth
Note: *The figure depicts a stylised view of long-run economic growth during 1870–1913. The average growth rate during 1870–1913 was 2 per cent per annum. The deviations about the long-run trend can be described as business cycle and long swing about the long-run trend of the economy.*

falling from 2.1 per cent per annum during the period 1856–99 to 1.3 per cent during 1899–1913 (see figure 1.2). The validity of this interpretation hinges on the usefulness of the compromise estimate of GDP to describe the macroeconomic behaviour of the pre-1913 era: the compromise estimate would be a useful approximation of the behaviour of the macroeconomy if two important conditions are satisfied:

- the three estimates of GDP are independent of each other and are of equal reliability; and
- the measurement errors between the three estimates are random.

Neither of these assumptions is valid: the various components of GDP are of different reliabilities and the errors are clearly not random. The climacteric observed in the compromise estimate is a statistical artifact and the explanation for it is to be found in the data construction methods rather than in the

7

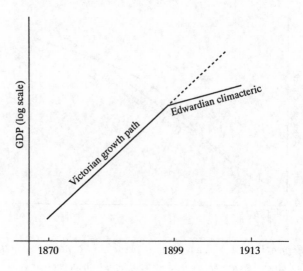

Figure 1.2: A stylised view of the UK climacteric
Note: *This figure depicts the UK growth path undergoing a structural break during 1899–1913 relative to the period 1856–99. While the rate of GDP growth had averaged 2 per cent per annum before 1899, during 1899–1913 the economy settled on a low growth path of 1.3 per cent per annum.*

true behaviour of the economy. The three estimates of GDP, considered individually, do not provide any evidence for a climacteric in the late nineteenth-century aggregate production trends: the output estimate shows steady growth throughout 1856–1913; the income and expenditure estimates follow a path of steady growth with a long swing pattern of alternating 'upswings' and 'downswings' of growth over shorter intervals. Thus, it is the simple averaging process used to construct the compromise estimate which is generating the observed climacteric in the macroeconomic data. In the light of these data problems, Solomou and Weale (1991) estimated a balanced measure of GDP to average the disaggregated component series.[2] The

---

[2] The main advantage of the balanced estimate of GDP over the compromise estimate is that the former uses information about the reliabilities of the disaggregated component series in constructing the estimate of aggregate GDP.

balanced series shows that long-run economic growth during 1899–1913 was comparable to the era 1873–90. A second line of criticism of the climacteric perspective can be found in the work of Crafts *et al.* (1989); using modern time series techniques to estimate the trend movement they argue that GDP followed a steady trend-stationary path over the period 1870–1913. Although some retardation was observed in the Edwardian period (1899–1913) this is best described as a mild long swing *cyclical* retardation, not a trend retardation.

In the light of this evidence a pertinent question to ask is, how successful was the interwar economy in returning to the pre-1913 growth path? We can glimpse at the changes taking place from the results reported in table 1.1: while UK GDP growth had averaged approximately 2 per cent per annum during 1870–1913, the long-run average growth rate for the period 1913–37 was only 1 per cent per annum. This can be represented as a transition to slower long-run economic growth as depicted in figure 1.3. A more realistic approximation to the changes taking place in the era 1913–37 can be seen from table 1.2. For most of the interwar period (1925–37) long-run output growth averaged 2 per cent per annum, a rate that is comparable to the pre-1913 epoch: adverse shocks accounting for the poor long-run performance during the long period 1913–37 are to be found in the trans-war period* of 1913–25 (Broadberry, 1990). This more detailed description of the growth process suggests that the shocks of the First World War and the immediate post-war reconstruction period* had *persistent* adverse effects on long-run macroeconomic performance. A stylised view of this is presented in figure 1.4. In the absence of the adverse shocks of the trans-war years the potential growth path of the macroeconomy would have yielded an output *level* that was significantly higher throughout the interwar era. This interpretation of the changes taking place in the period 1913–37 relative to 1870–1913 can be

Table 1.1. Long-term growth measures:
GDP, 1870–1937
(percent growth per annum)

1870–1913	2.0
1913–37	1.1

Source: Feinstein (1972).

Table 1.2. Medium-term growth measures:
GDP, 1913–37
(per cent growth per annum)

1913–25	0.0
1925–9	2.0
1929–37	2.0

Source: Feinstein (1972).

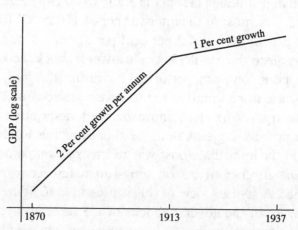

Figure 1.3: A first approximation to interwar economic growth
Note: *This figure illustrates that although the growth process generated
stable growth during 1870–1913, economic growth was not steady during
the interperiod comparisons of 1870–1937.*

10

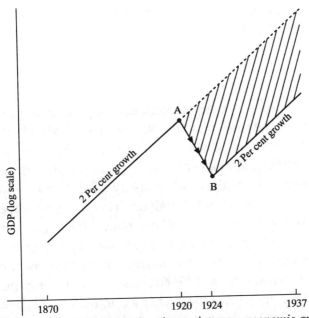

Figure 1.4: A second approximation to interwar economic growth
Note: *This figure illustrates that the shocks of the trans-war years (such as the war, the post-war inflation and the depression of 1920–1) had persistent adverse effects: a capacity gap, captured by the shaded area, existed throughout 1924–37. Average rates of economic growth were similar during 1870–1913 and 1924–37; however, the interwar economy operated around a low level equilibrium throughout the period.*

described in more technical language as a 'non-trend-stationary'* growth process: the post-1913 economy was unable to return to the pre-war growth path; instead, following from the trans-war shocks, aggregate output settled on a low level equilibrium that persisted throughout the interwar era.

Formal econometric tests for this persistence effect involve testing the hypothesis of a trend-stationary growth process. These econometric tests verify the conclusion we drew above that the pre-1913 economy grew along a trend-stationary macroeconomic path (Crafts *et al.* 1989). However, over the period 1870-1938 there is evidence of a break in this steady path, suggesting that the shocks of the trans-war years (1913–25)

11

displaced the pre-1913 steady growth path on a permanent basis (Mills, 1991).

CONCLUSIONS

Continuity and change in economic behaviour are features that are difficult to disentangle. Nevertheless, this brief overview of a number of perspectives suggests that there are enough aspects of discontinuity (although by no means representing independence from the past) to justify a focus on the interwar experience as a meaningful analytical exercise. Episodic events (such as the First World War), policy shifts (such as the decision to return to the pre-war gold standard arrangements) and changes in system characteristics pushed the economy on to a path that was quite different from the past. Thus, the kind of macroeconomic questions that we address in this book are meaningful for understanding the behaviour and performance of the UK interwar economy. For example, did the institutional changes introduced by state welfare systems and increased unionisation raise the equilibrium level of unemployment? Did the exchange rate regime constrain long-run economic performance? What were the new features accounting for increased output volatility in the interwar economy? Far from being misleading, the focus on the shocks determining the path of the interwar period is a useful exercise. Being useful, however, does not mean being complete. This approach should be treated as part of a broader picture that is needed to capture the complexities of historical processes.

APPENDIX A PICTORIAL SURVEY

This appendix provides long-run, time series plots of a number of important macroeconomic variables during the period

1870–1938. This should give the student a visual perspective to the interwar period in relation to the past.

GROSS DOMESTIC PRODUCT

Figure A.1 plots the compromise estimate of GDP during 1870–1938.

- The shocks of the immediate post-First World War period resulted in a shift of the trend level of aggregate output. The phrase 'segmented trend'* is often used to describe this feature: there is a clear break in the equilibrium path of the economy around 1919–21. In this sense the shocks of 1919–21 had a *persistent* effect on the equilibrium output level.
- The shocks of 1919–21 and the depression of 1929–32 meant that the macroeconomic volatility of the interwar era was greater than for the pre-1913 period. The variance of GDP is significantly higher in the interwar relative to the pre-1913 period.

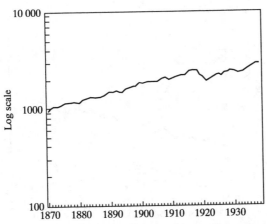

Figure 1A.1: Gross domestic product (constant 1900 prices: millions of £)

INDUSTRIAL PRODUCTION

Figure A.2 plots an index of industrial production for the period 1870–1938.

- The path of industrial production during the interwar period is more volatile than for the pre-1913 period.
- The shocks of 1919–21 are captured by the very large fall of industrial production during this period.
- The shocks of 1919–21 had a transitory cyclical effect on the industrial sector. The growth of industrial production during 1921–38 was sufficient to allow the series to return to the long-run path of the pre-shock period. This is in marked contrast to the path of GDP, which does not return to the pre-1913 trends.

AGRICULTURAL PRODUCTION

Figure A.3 plots the path of agricultural output during 1870–1938.

- The series is far more volatile in the pre-1913 period than during the interwar era. This is in marked contrast to the

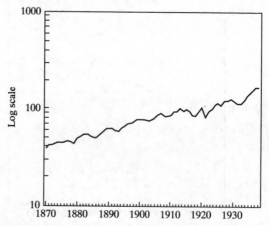

Figure 1A.2: Industrial production index (1913 = 100)

14

series for industrial production and gross domestic product.
• The pre-1913 series is marked by an absence of a trend, with downswings being followed by upswings. In contrast the interwar sees an upward trend in agricultural production.

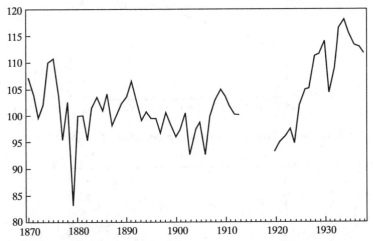

Figure 1A.3: Agricultural production, 1870–1938 (1913 = 100)

TRANSPORT AND COMMUNICATION
Figure A.4 plots the output index for the transport and communications sectors. Two features stand out:

• The pre-1913 trend is trend-stationary with a high mean growth rate of 2.7 per cent per annum.
• The trans-war years yield a major break in trend, which is reinforced by slower growth after 1920 (the mean growth between 1921–38 being 2.1 per cent).

DISTRIBUTION AND OTHER SERVICES
Figure A.5 plots the output index of distribution and services.

• The pre-1913 trend is trend-stationary with a mean growth rate of 1.9 per cent per annum.

15

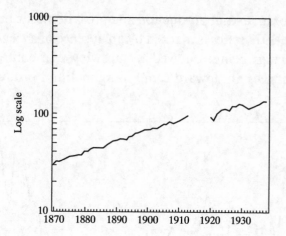

Figure 1A.4: Transport and communications, (1913 = 100)

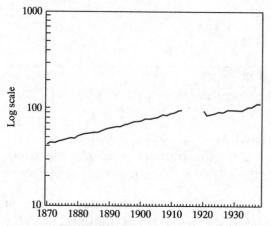

Figure 1A.5: Distribution services (1913 = 100)

- As with the transport and communication series a major break is observed in the trans-war period which is reinforced by slower growth during the 1920s and 1930s (the mean annual growth during 1921–38 averaged 0.9 per cent).

Given that the four activities (industrial production, agricultural production, transport and communications, and distribution

16

and services) provide a sectoral output decomposition of GDP it seems clear that the segmented break in GDP that we noted above needs to be explained by focusing on the latter two activities rather than the former two.

INVESTMENT

Figure A.6 plots gross domestic fixed capital formation for the period 1870–1938.

- The pre-1913 era is marked by long swings in the level of investment.
- The interwar period is marked by an upward trend in the level of investment.

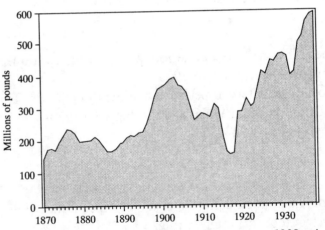

Figure 1A.6: Investment levels, 1870–1938 (constant 1938 prices)

PRICES

Figure A.7 plots the path of the GDP deflator*.

- Periods of deflation and inflation were observed before 1914, but the rates of change were quite low by interwar standards.

17

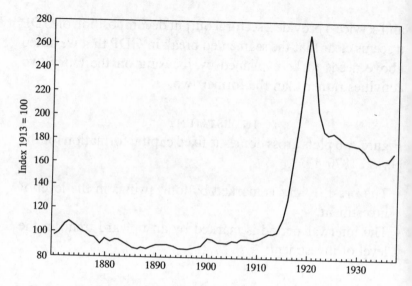

Figure 1A.7: Prices level, 1870–1937: GDP deflator (1913 = 100)

- The inflation of the war period was rapid and continued on a comparable path up to 1920.
- Most of the interwar period is marked by deflation. The rate of deflation is particularly sharp between 1920–3 and slows down during 1924–33.

NOMINAL INTEREST RATES

Figure A.8 plots nominal short-term (three monthly bills) and long-term (consol) interest rates.

- Interest rates during the early 1920s were historically relatively high.
- The 1930s saw a return to low interest rates, both in comparison to the 1920s and the classical gold standard period of 1870–1913.

18

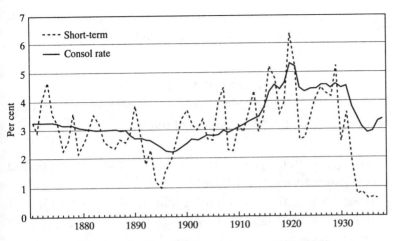

Figure 1A.8: Nominal interest rates, 1870–1938

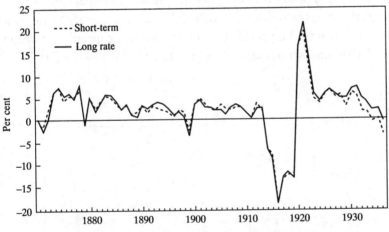

Figure 1A.9: Real interest rates, 1871–1937

REAL INTEREST RATES

Figure A.9 plots *ex post* real interest rates*, having made an adjustment for actual inflation rates.

- The unique high level of real interest rates in the early 1920s is more marked for real rates than nominal rates.

19

By the 1930s real interest rates returned to the mean levels observed during the classical gold standard period.

UNEMPLOYMENT RATE

Figure A.10 plots unemployment as a percentage of the labour force. Three distinctive features stand out:

- Average unemployment rates doubled in the interwar period compared to the pre-1913 era.
- Unemployment was highly cyclical: the depressions of 1920–21 and 1929–32 saw large rises in the rates of unemployment.
- Unemployment rates display the phenomenon of *persistence*: following the depression of 1920–1 unemployment rates fail to return to the pre-1920 level. It should be noted that in the 1930s unemployment rates did fall to the levels of 1929.

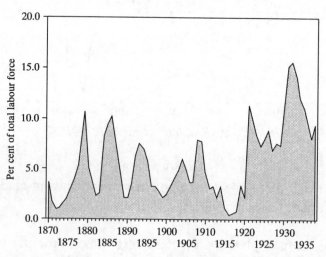

Figure 1A.10: Unemployment rate, 1870–1938 (per cent of labour force, 1870–1938)

20

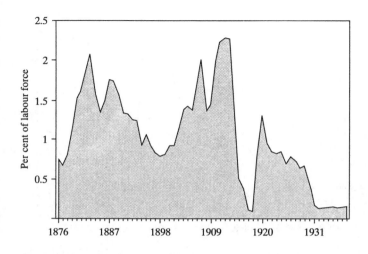

Figure 1A.11: Migration ratio, 1876–1938 (per cent of total labour force)

MIGRATION RATE

Figure A.11 plots external migration from the UK as a percentage of the labour force.

- Given the large level of migration before 1913 and its dependence on domestic economic pressures it may be interpreted as one of the adjustment mechanisms of the gold standard period. It seems to be the case that periods of slow economic growth at home (relative to overseas growth) stimulated migration.
- The stricter immigration rules of the New World during the interwar period significantly reduced the level of overseas migration from the UK. Thus, national specific shocks were increasingly being absorbed by adjustments to domestic unemployment rates rather than international migration flows.

21

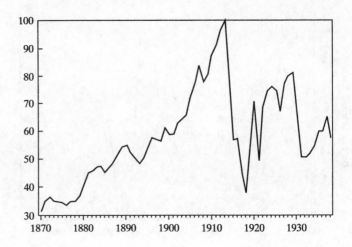

Figure A1.12: Volume of UK exports (1913 = 100)

EXPORTS

Figure A.12 plots UK exports in constant prices during 1870–1938.

- The trend growth path during 1870–1913 was segmented upwards with the rate of growth during 1870–99 being significantly lower than the rate observed during 1899–1913.
- The disruption of trade during the war resulted in a permanently lowered level of exports during the 1920s relative to the level of 1913.

- The world depression of the 1930s resulted in a further collapse of British exports.

SELECTED FURTHER READING

Kitson, M. and Solomou, S. (1990), *Protectionism and Economic Revival: The British Interwar Economy* (chapter 1).

Maddison, A. (1991), *Dynamic Forces in Capitalist Development* (chapter 4).

Eichengreen, B. (1994) 'The Inter-War Economy in A European Mirror', in Floud, R. and McCloskey, D.N., *The Economic History of Britain Since 1700*, Second Edition.

CHAPTER 2

THE EXCHANGE RATE REGIME AND UK ECONOMIC PERFORMANCE DURING THE 1920s

INTRODUCTION

During the 1920s UK economic performance lagged behind that of many other countries in the world economy. Much of the recent literature has attempted to explain this outcome in terms of the macroeconomic policy regime resulting from the return to a fixed exchange rate at the pre-war gold standard* parity (Moggridge, 1972; Broadberry, 1986; Eichengreen, 1992).

During 1870–1914 the value of the Pound was fixed relative to gold. America, France and Germany also sustained a fixed gold value for their currencies for most of this period (1879–1914), implying a fixed nominal exchange rate across the leading industrial economies. A restricted version of this system continued during the First World War: however, the large trade deficit and the low level of gold reserves in 1919 resulted in the formal abandonment of the gold standard by the UK in March of that year. Nevertheless, this significant change of policy was seen as a transitory measure: the aim of the government was to restore the gold standard to the pre-1913 parity as quickly as possible. This was achieved in the budget of 1925. There is now extensive evidence to suggest that the decision to return to the pre-1913 gold parity resulted in an overvaluation of the real exchange rate during the 1920s. This

24

overvaluation arose from two sources: first, countries such as Belgium, France and Italy chose not to return to the pre-1913 parity but instead returned to gold at a significantly depreciated rate; secondly, although the UK price level fell by more than many other countries between 1920 and 1925 the adjustment was not enough to allow the UK to return to the pre-1913 parity and maintain competitiveness, as implied by purchasing power parity theory*.

This chapter examines whether the exchange rate policy of the 1920s can be held *partly* responsible for the UK's economic problems after the First World War. First, it examines the evidence for the hypothesis that poor economic performance is associated with the exchange rate regime; secondly, it evaluates the extent and timing of overvaluation; finally, it examines various mechanisms through which possible adverse effects may have arisen.

EXCHANGE RATE REGIMES AND COMPARATIVE ECONOMIC PERFORMANCE

During the 1920s the economies of the industrialised world witnessed a variety of exchange rate policies. Table 2.1 summarises the exchange rate regimes of a number of the leading industrial economies: the USA was on the gold standard throughout the 1920s; some countries (such as the UK, Denmark, Norway and Sweden) left gold during the war or in the immediate post-war period, returning to the pre-1913 parity sometime in the mid 1920s; Belgium, France and Italy returned to gold in the 1920s but at a significantly depreciated exchange rate relative to the pre-1913 gold standard rate; others, such as Japan and Spain, allowed their currencies to float for longer, never returning to gold in the 1920s. These cross-country differences in exchange rate policies resulted in a variety of exchange rate experiences which can be compared to

Table 2.1. Flexible and fixed exchange rate periods

	Flexible	Fixed	Gold parity
UK	1919–25	1925–31	1913
Argentina	1919–27	1927–9	1913
Australia	1919–25	1925–9	1913
Austria	1919–23	1923–31	1913
Belgium	1919–25	1925–35	Depreciated
Canada	1919–26	1926–31	1913
Denmark	1919–27	1927–31	1913
France	1919–28	1928–36	Depreciated
Germany	1919–24	1924–31	1913
Italy	1919–27	1927–36	Depreciated
Japan	1919–30	1930–1	1913
Netherlands	1919–25	1925–36	1913
Norway	1919–28	1928–31	1913
Sweden	1919–24	1924–31	1913
United States	–	1919–33	1913

evaluate the effect of different exchange rate policies on national economic performance.

A number of existing studies provide a good starting point for this discussion. In a comparative analysis of the UK and the Scandinavian economies Broadberry (1984) argues that overvaluation caused poor economic performance in all these economies, as measured by high unemployment rates. Eichengreen (1986 and 1992) studies a larger cross-section of twelve countries during 1921–7 (UK, France, Norway, Sweden, Italy, Spain, Denmark, Holland, Canada, America, Australia and Japan) and finds a significant correlation between changes in exchange rates and changes in industrial production, with a depreciated exchange rate resulting in a higher growth rate for industrial production. Controlling for the magnitude of wartime disruption, countries that allowed their exchange rates to depreciate in the 1920s performed better than other countries.

Broadberry's work relates the exchange rate to unemployment for a very small group of countries. However, unemployment can be a poor indicator of economic performance, the Scandinavian economies being a good example of high unemployment and high economic growth during the 1920s. Eichengreen's work discusses the cyclical recovery during 1921–7; one (implicit) implication of his focus on the early phase of cyclical recovery is that the exchange rate did not have long-run effects. We will aim to show in the course of the analysis below that exchange rate policy had cyclical and more persistent effects. The remainder of this section will be devoted to extending the comparative methodology with the aim of distinguishing the impact of the exchange rate regime on comparative cyclical and long-run growth performance in the 1920s.

CYCLICAL RECOVERY PATHS AND EXCHANGE RATES

Figure 2.1 plots the cyclical recovery paths of gross domestic product for the major industrial economies. The specific phase of the cycle considered is the recovery from the shocks of the early 1920s to the end of the 1920s. Although UK cyclical recovery is near the bottom of the ranked distribution this cannot simply be attributed to the exchange rate regime: a multicausal framework is needed to capture the effect of the exchange rate, controlling for other important variables on cyclical recovery. If we simply attempt to evaluate the bivariate relationship between cyclical economic growth and the exchange rate we are likely to omit important variables from the discussion which, inevitably, will bias our results. Thus, Eichengreen considers the exchange rate in conjunction with the effects of wartime devastation on the level of production. The model below evaluates the cyclical effect of the exchange rate regime within a more general multivariate model for a group of major countries for which we have data (the variables

27

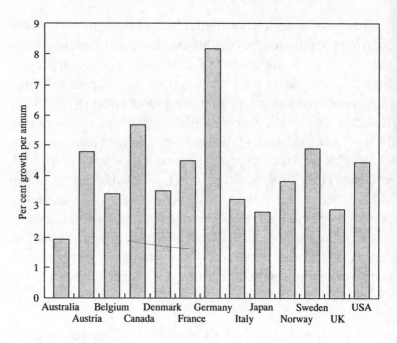

Figure 2.1: Cyclical growth in 1920s (per cent growth per annum)

are described in an appendix to this chapter, pp. 50–1).

$G_t = a + b$ long-run growth $+ c$ accelerationist $+ d$ start $+ e$
amplitude $+ f$ exchange rate regime $+ \varepsilon_t$ ... (1)

The results reported in table 2.2 distinguish the experience of France, Belgium and Italy from other countries because they allowed their nominal exchange rates to depreciate relative to the pre-1913 gold parity. The results fail to distinguish an effect from the nominal exchange rate to the cyclical growth performance.

One reason for this result is that amongst the group of countries pursuing policies of returning to gold at the pre-1913 parity some were more competitive than others, reflecting long-run economic performance and the differential impact of the First World War. There is little evidence of the exchange

Table 2.2. Explaining the cross-sectional cyclical recovery in the 1920s: regression estimates (t–*values in parentheses*)

Parameter	Estimated co-efficient	t-ratio
$\hat{a}$	1.96	(0.60)
$\hat{b}$	1.58	(2.59)
$\hat{c}$	1.73	(2.23)
$\hat{d}$	−0.04	−(1.55)
$\hat{e}$	−0.13	−(1.80)
$\hat{f}$	1.42	(1.24)

$\bar{R}^2 = 0.52$

Notes: Model estimated:
Cyclical growth $= a + b$ long-run growth $+ c$ acceleration $+ d$ start $+ e$ amplitude $+ f$ nominal exchange rate regime dummy $+ \varepsilon_t$.
Dummy $= 1$ for depreciating economies (Belgium, France and Italy).

rate being overvalued in America, Japan or Sweden (Eichengreen, 1992) while there is extensive evidence of overvaluation in the UK, Germany and Norway. America was on gold at the 1913 parity throughout 1919–29 and hence did not face the costly adjustment path of leaving and returning to gold; Japan did not join the gold standard until 1930; although Sweden joined early in 1924 its price level was competitive. Thus, another feature of the exchange rate that needs to be considered is the level of competitiveness as measured by the real exchange rate. Table 2.3 distinguishes the real exchange rate experience of France, Belgium, Italy, the USA, Japan and Sweden from that of the overvalued currencies. The fit of the above model, as measured by R^2, improves from 0.52 to 0.65. Countries with competitive real exchange rates in the 1920s performed better than other countries.

Summarising so far, countries depreciating their currencies did not perform better than other countries in the cyclical recovery of the 1920s. A depreciated exchange rate was

Table 2.3. Explaining the cross-sectional cyclical recovery in the 1920s: regression estimates (t–*values in parentheses*)

Parameter	Estimated co-efficient	t-ratio
$\hat{a}$	4.44	(2.24)
$\hat{b}$	1.29	(2.97)
$\hat{c}$	1.44	(2.17)
$\hat{d}$	−0.06	−(2.94)
$\hat{e}$	−0.17	−(2.55)
$\hat{f}$	1.60	(2.18)
$\bar{R}^2 = 0.65$		

Notes: Model estimated:
Cyclical growth = $a + b$ long-run growth + c acceleration + d start + e amplitude + f real exchange rate regime dummy + ε_t.
Dummy = 1 for Belgium, France, Italy, USA, Japan and Sweden.

sufficient but not *necessary* to maintain competitiveness. The cyclical recovery paths of France, Belgium and Italy are indistinguishable from countries that did not see a long-term depreciation of their currencies (such as America, Japan and Sweden). In the case of the UK, given the adverse effects of the First World War (in terms of a loss of markets) it would seem sensible to argue that for the UK to maintain international competitiveness in the 1920s, a depreciated exchange rate would have been a necessary feature of a more successful UK cyclical recovery.

LONG-RUN ECONOMIC PERFORMANCE AND THE EXCHANGE RATE REGIME

Figure 2.2 plots the interperiod growth changes of GDP between 1913–29 and 1870–1913 as a percentage of the growth rate between 1870–1913. The UK long-run growth rate for the period 1913–29 fell by 60 per cent relative to that in the period 1870–1913. In order to determine whether there is a significant

30

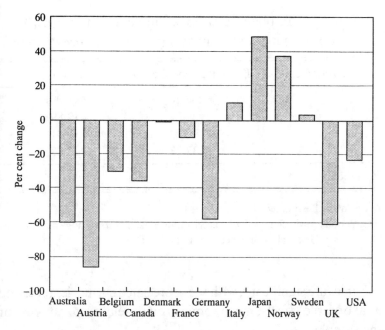

Figure 2.2: Growth performance in 1920s (per cent interperiod change)

exchange rate effect on the differences shown in figure 2.2 the following model was estimated:

$$\frac{\Delta G_t}{G_t} = a + b \text{ accelerationist} + c \text{ start} + d \text{ exchange rate}$$
$$\text{regime} + \varepsilon_t \tag{2}$$

The dependent variable measures the percentage interperiod growth change over 1913–29 relative to 1870–1913 for a cross-section of countries. The independent variables are the same as those defined above. The exchange rate regime variable distinguishes the experience of countries whose nominal exchange rate depreciated (Belgium, France and Italy) from the rest of the sample. The results of table 2.4 show that the model accounts for over 80 per cent of growth changes; all the

31

Table 2.4. Explaining cross-sectional long-run growth
variations: regression estimates (t–*values in parentheses*)

Parameter	Estimated co-efficient	t-ratio
$\hat{a}$	−262.20	−(8.09)
$\hat{b}$	27.27	(2.89)
$\hat{c}$	2.22	(6.91)
$\hat{d}$	32.33	(2.87)
$\bar{R}^2 = 0.83$		

Notes: Model estimated:
Inter-period growth change = $a + b$ acceleration + c start + d exchange rate dummy.
Dummy = 1 for Belgium, France and Italy.

variables are significant, with the depreciated currencies receiving
a favourable effect on economic growth relative to the rest of
the sample.

Countries that saw depreciated nominal exchange rates in
the 1920s, relative to the pre-1913 gold standard parity,
received a favourable long-run stimulus relative to other
countries. At first sight this result seems paradoxical with the
earlier finding that nominal depreciation did not give Belgium,
France and Italy a stronger cyclical recovery during the 1920s.
One way to account for this paradoxical result is within the
framework of output hysteresis: countries returning to the gold
standard at the pre-1913 parity suffered a persistent adverse
output effect in the attempt to reestablish the old parity. These
relative paths are presented in a stylised form in figure 2.3. For
simplicity the figure assumes that during the pre-1913 period
both sets of countries grew at a comparable rate. The
comparative growth rate is also similar after the shocks of the
early 1920s. However, because the shocks of 1913–24 are worse
and persistent for the countries returning to the pre-1913
parity, long-run growth comparisons are better for the

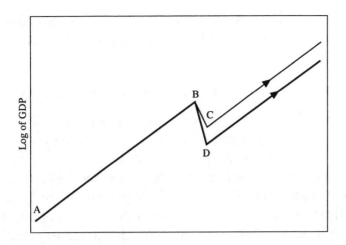

Figure 2.3: Persistence effects: a stylised view

Note: *Along path AB both groups of countries grew at a similar rate. Countries attempting to make a fast transition to returning to the pre-1913 gold parity saw more severe depression during 1920–1 than countries allowing for a more gradualist approach. Although both sets of countries grew along similar paths during the recovery period of the 1920s, the shocks of 1920–1 had persistent effects on the level of output throughout the 1920s.*

depreciating countries. The causes of this persistent output effect are discussed at the end of this chapter.

SUMMARY AND QUESTIONS

- Distinguishing between short-run cyclical performance and long-run economic growth performance is vital in analysing the effects of exchange rates during the 1920s. The level of the nominal exchange rate had persistent effects on equilibrium output. What were the mechanisms by which the reestablishment of the pre-1913 gold parity constrained economies in the long run?
- The level of international competitiveness, as measured by the real exchange rate, was important to cyclical recovery paths. What evidence is there that the UK was burdened with an

overvalued real exchange rate in the 1920s, and what were the mechanisms by which this gave rise to poor cyclical recovery?

THE EXTENT OF UK OVERVALUATION

Ever since Keynes' *The Economic Consequences of Mr Churchill* it has been widely accepted by economic historians that, when the UK returned to the gold standard in 1925, sterling was overvalued by at least 10 per cent relative to the dollar. In order to determine the magnitude of overvaluation we need to consider the theory of exchange rate determination. The theory used by Keynes and in most of the recent empirical analyses of this issue is purchasing power parity (PPP) theory*. PPP theory begins with the premise that, in equilibrium, a flexible exchange rate reflects movements in relative prices between countries. If prices rise in the UK relative to the USA by 10 per cent (reducing UK competitiveness), to maintain equilibrium in the international accounts the pound is expected to depreciate relative to the dollar by 10 per cent. A flexible exchange rate mechanism, with efficient exchange rate markets, should yield this outcome.

Two important issues need to be considered: first, was the UK exchange rate overvalued at the time of the return to gold in 1925; second, since the exchange rate market is an asset market that adjusts relatively quickly to market news (such as policy announcements) did the policy announcements in 1919 of the intention of returning to the pre-1913 gold standard have the effect of appreciating the real exchange rate at some point between 1919 and 1925. Given high UK inflation after the First World War, relative to the USA, the announcement of a future return to the gold standard was equivalent to an announcement of a contractionary monetary policy to deflate the price level. A contractionary monetary policy is expected to depress domestic output (thus reducing imports and improving

34

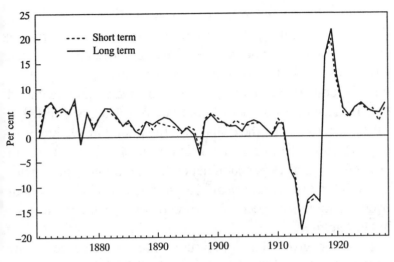

Figure 2.4: Real interest rates, 1873–1931

the balance of trade) by raising the level of domestic real interest rates* (which improves the capital account of the balance of payments). The exceptional height of real interest rates during 1921–3 is documented in figure 2.4. As a result under the flexible exchange rate regime of 1919–25 contractionary monetary policy is expected to result in an appreciation of the nominal exchange rate. The contractionary monetary policy is also expected to deflate the price level, improving competitiveness. However, because the exchange rate is determined in an asset market that adjusts relatively quickly to market news, compared to the goods market, we would expect to observe a significant appreciation of the real exchange rate in the short run (often referred to as the phenomenon of exchange rate 'overshooting') whereby the exchange rate deviates from the PPP equilibrium (Dornbusch, 1976).

WAS STERLING OVERVALUED IN THE 1920s?

Real exchange rate movements can be calculated on a bilateral (two-country) or an effective (multilateral) exchange rate basis.

35

For countries on gold at the 1913 parity (such as the USA and the UK) calculating the level of the real exchange rate is equivalent to comparing their relative price movements between 1913 and 1925. The bilateral comparisons do not give an unambiguous answer to the question of overvaluation. Redmond (1984) presents a number of comparisons which suggest that PPP calculations for the dollar and the pound in 1925 relative to 1913 range from an undervaluation of 4 per cent to an overvaluation of 17 per cent, depending on which type of price index is used for comparison. Keynes' result of a 10 per cent overvaluation is a special outcome of the specific retail price indices he used.

However, given that individual countries returned to the gold standard at different dates in the 1920s, and that some chose to return at much depreciated exchange rates relative to those in 1913, bilateral exchange rates* with other pre-1913 gold parity countries (such as the USA) will not be a representative measure of overall competitiveness. A more representative indicator of competitiveness is the real multilateral exchange rate*, which measures both nominal exchange rate variations and relative price movements for a wide sample of UK trading partners. Such an effective exchange rate is constructed by weighting the basket of bilateral exchange rates of the main UK trading partners.[1] Table 2.5 presents a number of calculations for 1924–30. The evidence shows that by this measure, the UK exchange rate was overvalued in 1925 by between 5 and 20 per cent: only the magnitude of overvaluation remains conditional on the type of price index used. Since the effective exchange rate contains far more information about UK competitiveness than does the bilateral rate with the US,

---

[1] Weights can be calculated either on a bilateral basis (between Britain and another country) or on a multilateral basis (using world trade shares as weights). The former captures direct trade links while the latter recognises that competition can take place in 'third markets', rather than directly between two countries.

Table 2.5. Multilateral real effective exchange rate for the pound, 1924–30 (1913=100)

	Deflating by wholesale prices[a]	Deflating by retail prices[b]
1924	95.2	83.4
1925	94.8	79.6
1926	92.0	73.8
1927	97.3	81.5
1928	98.5	81.9
1929	101.3	84.9
1930	103.5	87.2

Notes:
[a] A trade weighted index for 19 countries.
[b] A trade weighted index for 16 countries.
 The series are constructed so that a number below 100 represent overvaluation (relative to 1913).
Source: Redmond (1984).

there is strong evidence to suggest that sterling returned to gold at an overvalued parity in 1925 relative to 1913.

To use PPP theory to evaluate the equilibrium level of the exchange rate in the 1920s we need some initial benchmark year for comparison. Since our aim was to measure the changes after the First World War relative to the past, 1913 was used on this assumption. But how normal was 1913 in terms of the real effective exchange rate of the pre-war period? The real exchange rate during the classical gold standard varied for a number of reasons: first, a number of UK trading partners were not on gold during this period, leading to variations in the nominal effective exchange rate; second, the real exchange rate within the gold countries might have varied as a result of differential price and productivity movements across countries (Balassa, 1964). In order to shed some light on the longer-run behaviour of the UK real effective exchange rate consider figure 2.5 which

37

plots the UK real effective rate during the pre-1913 period (Solomou and Catao, 1994). Quite clearly 1913 is not 'normal' if that means that it represents the long-run mean level of the nominal or real effective exchange rate of the gold standard era. In fact 1913 represents a low point in the level of the real effective exchange rate during the period 1870–1913. The question that needs to be addressed if 1913 is to be used as the benchmark year for comparison is how permanent would the level of the exchange rate of that year have been, in the absence of the First World War? Comparing the level of the real exchange rate in the 1920s with 1900 as a benchmark, the case for overvaluation is significantly reduced.

In addition, the PPP model is only one amongst a number of models of exchange rate determination. An example of an alternative perspective is provided by Matthews' (1989) supply-side theory of the exchange rate. In this model the high 'replacement ratio'[2] (resulting from a generous benefits system) is assumed to have pushed up UK wage costs relative to other countries. A high replacement ratio increases search unemployment, forcing employers to bid up real wages* to attract workers away from leisure: the exchange rate simply reflected the adjustment to supply-side shocks in the UK labour market. In this sense we cannot speak of an 'overvaluation' of the exchange rate; the distortion is to be found in the institutions of the labour market. To improve UK competitiveness would have required a reduction in the replacement ratio to induce more flexibility in the labour market.

As a model of the exchange rate this provides a consistent alternative theoretical framework to PPP theory. This model of exchange rate determination can only be appropriately tested within an international context, since the rise in the

---

[2] The 'replacement ratio' refers to the ratio of average benefits to average wages as an influence on the intertemporal decision between work and leisure. The concept is discussed further in the chapter on unemployment.

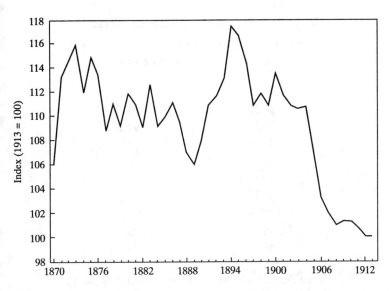

Figure 2.5: Real effective exchange rate, 1870–1913 (1913 = 100)

replacement ratio was a common feature amongst a number of industrial countries in the interwar period; hence, only the *differential* in the rise in the replacement ratio across countries might be expected to influence competitiveness. Moreover, as is shown in the discussion of unemployment (chapter 3) it is not clear that the replacement ratio had a large impact on UK wage costs or unemployment. Much more research needs to be undertaken on these supply-side influences at an international level of comparison before this is regarded as a convincing framework for understanding interwar problems.

We also need to consider the effect of policy announcements in 1919 concerning the return to gold. Table 2.6 presents various exchange rate calculations for this earlier period. The real effective exchange rate is actually significantly more overvalued in the policy announcement period of 1920–1 than in 1925. Thus, the *impact effects* of exchange rate movements were already important in the cyclical depression

39

Table 2.6. Multilateral real UK effective
exchange rates (January 1924 = 100)

1920	110.8
1921	107.2
1922	94.6
1923	98.7
1924	102.5
1925	103.3
1926	103.2
1927	97.3
1928	95.8
1929	95.2
1930	94.1

Note: The series is constructed so that as the exchange
rate appreciates the index rises.
Source: Andrews (1982) quoted in Broadberry (1986).

of 1920–1, long before the return to the gold standard in 1925
(Broadberry, 1990). Since this depression was extremely serious
and had persistent effects on economic performance the focus
of the literature on overvaluation in 1925 is rather misleading.
The impact of exchange rate movements in the 1920–1
depression is discussed further in the chapter on business
cycles.

EXCHANGE RATES AND ECONOMIC PERFORMANCE

The cross-sectional evidence reported above distinguished an
exchange rate effect both on cyclical and longer-run economic
performance. This section discusses possible causal frameworks
to account for these observations, focusing on the experience
of the UK.

40

CYCLICAL ECONOMIC PERFORMANCE

The short-term effects of overvaluation in the 1920s have been extensively analysed using the elasticities approach to the balance of payments (Moggridge, 1972; Broadberry, 1986). This is a partial equilibrium approach that looks at the variation of the exchange rate (as a price variable) while making *ceteris paribus* assumptions about incomes and money. The price effects of an overvalued exchange rate are expected to lead to an adverse effect on the balance of trade. Consider, for example, the supply of UK exports to the USA, expressed in foreign currency (see figure 2.6). The overvalued exchange rate will reduce the demand for UK products by America and thus produce an inward shift in the supply of UK exports. The total change in foreign exchange earnings when we compare equilibria A and B is clearly dependent on the elasticity of demand for UK products (η_x) by America:

if, $\eta_x > 1$ foreign exchange earnings fall

$\eta_x = 1$ foreign exchange earnings are unchanged

$\eta_x < 1$ foreign exchange earnings rise

By a similar argument the overvaluation will make imports attractive shifting the UK demand for US products to the right (see figure 2.7). Thus, the demand for foreign exchange in this case rises. The overall effect on the balance of trade can be analysed in terms of the Marshall-Lerner elasticities condition. This predicts that the balance of trade will deteriorate with an overvaluation if the *sum* of the home price elasticity of demand for imports (η_m) and the foreign price elasticity of demand for exports (η_x) is greater than unity (assuming, for simplicity, perfectly elastic supply conditions in both the home and foreign markets). Moggridge (1972) shows that the Marshall-Lerner condition was satisfied during the interwar period with elasticity estimates of

41

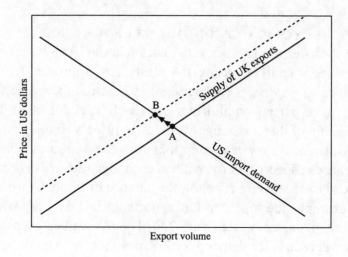

Figure 2.6: UK export volumes to the US

$$\eta_x = -1.5$$
$$\eta_m = -0.5$$

Thus, we can conclude that the overvaluation adversely affected the balance of trade.

To derive the magnitude of this effect we need to know more about the actual pricing strategy of importers and exporters in response to the change in the exchange rate (what are also known as the 'pass-through' properties of the overvaluation). The evidence we considered above showed that the overvaluation was in the range of 5 to 25 per cent relative to 1913. Moggridge calculated an overvaluation of 11 per cent, which is slightly below the mid-point of this range. The assumption of an 11 per cent overvaluation only measures the *potential* change in competitiveness; the actual change will be influenced by the pass-through pricing behaviour of importers and exporters. Since exporters are adversely affected by the overvaluation, Moggridge assumes that they were forced to take a cut in profit margins in an attempt to maintain competitiveness. Importers,

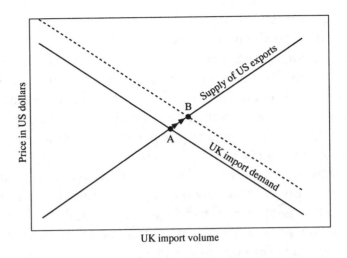

Figure 2.7: UK import volumes from the US

on the other hand, were favoured by a rise in demand and are assumed to have raised mark-ups. Thus, it is assumed that the dollar price of exports rose only by 7 per cent (i.e., the sterling price of exports fell by 4 per cent) and the dollar price of imports rose by 3 per cent (i.e., the sterling price of imports fell by only 8 per cent and not by the full 11 per cent overvaluation). With these pass-through assumptions and the estimated elasticities of demand, the balance of trade deteriorated by £80m. Moggridge calculates that 750,000 jobs were lost as a result of the overvalued exchange rate.

Moggridge's approach shows that the balance of trade effect of the overvaluation generated adverse effects on income and employment. However, it would be misleading to accept the numbers at face value, or to see this as the only mechanism by which UK economic performance was hindered. The model yielding the numbers is based on statistical estimates with a margin of error (e.g., the price elasticities of demand) and assumptions which have not been tested (e.g., the pass-through assumptions). More generally the partial equilibrium approach of the elasticities framework neglects many other macroeconomic effects of overvaluation. We will discuss these aspects below when we consider long-run growth performance, but a brief mention should be made of them here. First, overvaluation will have an effect on the overall macroeconomic policy regime. A fixed exchange rate, by its nature, restricts the government's use of discretionary monetary policy to influence the level of demand; an overvalued fixed exchange rate constrains the government to maintain a high interest rate policy to sustain the credibility of remaining on the gold standard.[3] Thus, the economy was burdened with high nominal and real interest rates throughout the 1920s: real interest rates were historically unprecedented throughout the 1920s.

The effect on the labour market also needs to be considered. One of the features of the 1920s is that countries that left the gold standard during the trans-war period* (1913–24), and chose to return to the 1913 parity, had to pursue persistent restrictive monetary policies to bring the price level down relative to the early post-war period. Thus, the UK saw a rate of price deflation that was much higher than countries not returning to the 1913 parity (such as France, Belgium and Italy). Given the institutional rigidity of labour markets, a phenomenon that had its roots in the pre-1914 period, contractionary monetary policy resulted in a deflated price level, giving a real-wage level that was above that of the more competitive exchange rate countries. Thus, the level of unemployment in the overvalued countries was relatively high in the 1920s (Broadberry, 1984).

LONG-RUN PERSISTENT EFFECTS

Countries that returned to the gold standard at the 1913 parity

---

[3] The overvalued exchange rate also had adverse fiscal impacts. A lower exchange rate (resulting in a higher national income) would have improved the budget deficit and, if the government had followed the balanced budget rule of the time, it could have increased expenditure or cut taxes which would have given a further boost to income and employment (Hatton, 1988).

performed worse in the long run than countries which depreciated their currencies. The explanation for this adverse effect on economic growth is at least partly to be found in the persistent adverse effects of exchange rate variations in the early post-First World War reconstruction period. We now consider a number of persistence mechanisms that arose out of the exchange rate shocks of the early post-war period of 1919–21.

THE EXCHANGE RATE AND INTEREST RATES

Although the government did not intervene directly in the exchange rate market between 1919–25 it did so indirectly via monetary policy. In order to achieve the exchange rate target of the pre-1913 gold parity the government pursued a contractionary monetary policy during 1920–5. During 1913–20 the UK inflation rate rose faster than that of America and had to be brought more in line for a successful return to the 1913 parity. The greatest impact of the tight monetary policy was observed during 1921–3 with exceptionally high real interest rates. When the pre-war parity was reestablished in 1925 at an overvalued exchange rate, monetary policy had to be used to sustain the exchange rate target. High real and nominal interest rates persisted throughout the period 1920–31.[4] Moreover, one of the pillars of the credibility of the gold standard was balanced budgets; hence, in line with economic ideology at the time, the government could not expand the economy via the use of fiscal policy. High interest rates prevented the potential expansion of interest-sensitive sectors such as housing (Broadberry, 1986).

EXCHANGE RATES AND PRICES

The price deflation of countries returning to gold at the pre-1913 parity was rapid. The full implication of this deflation on economic growth has to be linked to the immediate

---

[4] Real interest rates during 1924–9 averaged 5.5 per cent. Two other peaks are observed in the long-run data: during 1873–82 and 1980–93 real interest rates have averaged 4.5 per cent.

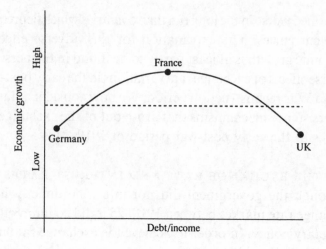

Figure 2.8: Debt–income ratios and economic performance

post-war boom of 1918–20. In the expectation of a prosperous future, with weakened German competition, the staple export sectors in the UK (iron and steel, textiles, shipbuilding, coal) increased their level of debt to finance much needed investment. However, the era of prosperity did not materialise: the permanent deflation of 1920–2 left these industries with a large real debt-burden. Given the government's commitment to the lower price level, new investment by existing firms was held back as they struggled to meet large debt repayments under conditions of poor export performance and high import penetration. Table 2.7 shows the level of the aggregate debt to income ratio for a group of countries in 1913 and 1929. The UK was burdened with a relatively high debt to income ratio. Figure 2.8 depicts the relationship between real debt and economic growth as a non-linear one. The level of real debt in Germany and Austria was even lower than that observed in France, Belgium and Italy: yet, economic performance in both these economies was poor in the 1920s. Hyperinflation had eliminated most of the nominal debt but at the same time it

46

Table 2.7. Debt–income ratios, 1913–29

	UK	France	Belgium	Italy
1913	1.6	2.8	1.7	1.3
1929	2.8	2.1	1.4	1.3

Source: Goldsmith (1984)

weakened domestic financial institutions so much that the provision of new domestic credit was seriously constrained.

EXCHANGE RATES AND IMPORTS

One interpretation of poor economic performance in the UK is the persistent adverse effect of the cyclical depression of 1921. The largest overvaluation of the real exchange rate occurred in 1920–2 (Broadberry, 1986). A persistent adverse effect arose from this overvaluation as foreign firms penetrated the UK market on a permanent basis. Even though the magnitude of overvaluation fell between 1922–9 economic growth did not return to old trends because the nature of competition had changed. Once foreign firms had established distribution networks in the UK, changes in the exchange rate were not enough to reestablish the original equilibrium. Moreover, we should note that many of the countries penetrating the UK market had stronger supply-side potential than the domestic economy.[5] As is shown in figure 2.9 the import ratio increased in the early 1920s and remained persistently high throughout the 1920s. It took the policy regime change of protection and devaluation in the 1930s to reverse this path (Kitson and Solomou, 1990).

[5] This includes better training and education, more flexible labour markets and technologically advanced industries.

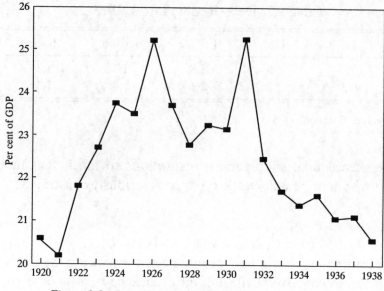

Figure 2.9: Import ratio, 1920–38 (per cent of GDP)

HOW LONG IS THE LONG RUN?

The evidence we have discussed in this chapter suggests that the return to the gold standard at the pre-1913 parity constrained the cyclical and long-run performance of the UK economy. This conclusion is, however, limited to an analysis of the recovery path of the 1920s; these policy issues take on a more complex dimension if we extend the analysis of the policy impact into the 1930s. The countries that benefited from depreciation in the 1920s (France, Italy and Belgium) had done so at high social costs: the inflationary path of these economies resulted in large changes in income distribution that generated a very strong fear of inflation in the collective memory, limiting policy actions in the 1930s. The fear of inflation meant that the option of devaluation was not a politically viable policy in these countries. Hence, they became locked into maintaining the gold standard under the adverse conditions of the 1930s.

48

The result was economic stagnation in the 1930s. On the other hand, countries that achieved price stability in the 1920s, as a means of returning to the 1913 gold parity, were (paradoxically) able to shift policy in the 1930s in response to the new circumstances of world depression. It is, thus, important to realise that, although the exchange rate regime of the 1920s had adverse effects on the UK economy, the policy implications of this finding are not clear. To the extent that policy should serve the purpose of sustaining long-run economic growth, returning to gold at the 1913 parity had some rationale: the aim was to institute a credible policy to control inflation. This it did. In doing so this created policy flexibility for the future (even though that was clearly not the initial intention). By gaining credibility governments could sacrifice this inflation credibility to generate some revival from the world depression. In a world of uncertainty this policy flexibility was essential for coping with the adverse shocks of the 1930s. On the other hand, the unintended policy flexibility in the 1930s was bought at a high price in the 1920s.

CONCLUSIONS

- The nominal exchange rate influenced long-run economic performance via a persistent effect on output in the early 1920s. The real exchange rate influenced cyclical economic performance, with the overvalued countries performing worse than the more competitive economies.
- The exchange rate policy of returning to the pre-1913 gold parity constrained economic performance during the 1920s. However, in the medium term, the policies of the 1920s gave the UK the (unanticipated) policy flexibility to leave the gold standard and shift towards an expansionary monetary policy in response to the adverse shocks of the early 1930s. The countries that gained from a depreciated currency in the

1920s had done so with the high social costs of inflation, leading to political stalemate on new policy options during the 1930s.

- There does not exist a successful role model that the UK should have followed: the path of the depreciating currencies resulted in social costs in the 1920s and constraints in the 1930s; the path of the overvalued currencies resulted in more immediate constraints in the 1920s. The shocks of the First World War and the immediate post-war period required a policy response: neither large depreciation nor returning to the pre-1913 parities were appropriate responses. In the light of modern economic theory and ex-post observation we can prescribe policies that would have performed better, but they may be unrealistic given the degree of international policy co-ordination that was possible in the 1920s.

APPENDIX   VARIABLE DESCRIPTION

LONG-RUN GROWTH RATE

This is the long-run growth rate observed between 1870 and 1913. The economies which then grew rapidly are expected to have had relatively fast growth in the 1920s. For example, America averaged 4 per cent aggregate growth per annum between 1870 and 1913 while UK growth averaged less than 2 per cent. We might therefore expect the average GDP growth rate of America to have been potentially higher than that of the UK. This is a variable to make more comparable the scale of different national growth paths.

ACCELERATION

A large group of countries experienced accelerating output growth during 1870–1913, resulting possibly from a catching-up growth process. If the supply potential of an economy is generating fast and accelerating output growth, cyclical recovery might be at faster rates than in countries which had experienced more stable trend-stationary economic growth before 1914 (for example the UK, USA, Canada, Australia). A dummy variable (1 = accelerationist, 0 = other) captures these different experiences.

START

This is the level of GDP in the early 1920s relative to that in 1913, to capture the effect of wartime disruptions. There could be a number of theories about the direction of this effect. A catching-up theory would argue that, if the disruptions were large, there would be fast cyclical recovery.

AMPLITUDE

The 'start' variable captures the size of the required adjustment of the economy to wartime disruption. We also need to consider the impact of short-run shocks from depression in the early 1920s. Thus, 'amplitude' is the peak to trough movement of depression in the early 1920s

EXCHANGE RATE REGIME

A dummy variable (1 = depreciated, 0 = other) is used to compare the depreciated currencies (France, Belgium and Italy) relative to other countries.

SELECTED FURTHER READING

Comparative studies

Broadberry, S.N. (1984), 'The North European Depression in the 1920s', *Scandinavian Economic History Review*.

Eichengreen, B. (1986), 'Understanding 1921–1927: Inflation and Economic Recovery in the 1920s', *Revista di Storia Economica*.

UK focused studies

Broadberry, S.N. (1986), *The British Economy Between the Wars* (chapter 12).

Dimsdale, N.H. (1981), 'British Monetary Policy and the Exchange Rate 1920–1938', in Eltis, W.A. and Sinclair, P.J.N. (eds.).

Matthews, K.G.P. (1986), 'Was Sterling Overvalued in 1925?', *Economic History Review*.

Moggridge, D.E. (1972), *British Monetary Policy, 1924–31: The Norman Conquest of $4.86*.

Redmond, J. (1984), 'The Sterling Overvaluation in 1925: A Multilateral Approach', *Economic History Review*.

CHAPTER 3

UNEMPLOYMENT, 1919–38

INTRODUCTION

Perhaps the most distinguishing feature of the interwar era was the rise of mass unemployment. Figure 3.1 plots the path of the annual UK unemployment rate during the period 1890–1938. Total unemployment as a percentage of the labour force more than doubled from an average of 4.5 per cent between 1870 and 1913 to nearly 10 per cent between 1920 and 1938 (see appendix to this chapter for a description of the data). The unemployment rate had reached the 10 per cent mark in the past but only over short time periods. There are three important features to note: first, unemployment showed a very marked cyclical pattern during 1918–38, rising rapidly in the severe depressions of 1920–1 and 1929–32 and falling in the recovery periods of 1921–9 and 1932–7. Secondly, figure 3.1 suggests that the severity of the problem was worsening within the interwar years: with each major cyclical depression the unemployment rate rose to ever higher levels. Finally, the level of unemployment displays the phenomenon of hysteresis*, whereby the mean rate of unemployment was permanently higher in the interwar years relative to the pre-1914 era.

The problem of high and rising unemployment during this period was not limited to the UK economy. However, international comparisons are difficult to make because of

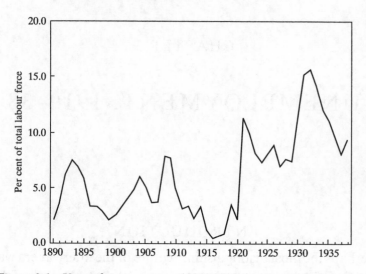

Figure 3.1: Unemployment rates, 1890–1938 (per cent of labour force)

national inconsistencies in the definition and measurement o
unemployment (Eichengreen and Hatton, 1988). Two importan
pieces of work that have attempted to grapple with these
problems of data comparability are Galenson and Zellner
(1957) and Maddison (1964): the Galenson and Zellner data
may be regarded as an indicator of the *ranking* of industria
unemployment levels across a wide range of countries, while
Maddison provides comparable aggregate unemploymen
figures. These comparative figures, presented in table 3.1
suggest that the UK was a relatively high unemploymen
economy throughout the interwar years. In the 1920s UK
industrial unemployment was the highest amongst all the
major industrial countries. The UK experience in the 1920s
was not, however, unique: industrial unemployment rates were
also high in the Scandinavian economies (Denmark, Norway
and Sweden) and Germany. In the 1930s the world situation
changed markedly; while the UK remained a high unemployment
economy many other countries also manifested historically
unprecedented unemployment rates. This chapter explains the

Table 3.1. Average unemployment rates (%) 1921–38

	Industrial unemployment		Total unemployment	
	1921–29	1930–38	1921–29	1930–38
Major industrial countries				
France	3.8	10.2	–	–
Germany	9.2	21.8	4.0	8.8
UK	12.0	15.4	6.8	9.8
USA	7.7	26.1	4.9	18.2
Other industrial countries				
Belgium	2.4	14.0	1.5	8.7
Denmark	18.7	21.9	4.5	6.6
Netherlands	8.3	24.3	2.4	8.7
Norway	16.8	26.6	–	–
Sweden	14.2	16.8	3.4	5.6

Source: Industrial unemployment rates from Galenson and Zellner (1957) and Lebergott (1964). Total unemployment rates from Maddison (1964).

high and persistent rise of unemployment in this period within a number of theoretical frameworks.

THEORETICAL EXPLANATIONS OF UNEMPLOYMENT

This section provides an overview of a number of models that will be used to evaluate the historical evidence.

THE AUCTION MARKET FOR LABOUR

The auction market* theory of the labour market is one of the oldest theories and has had a major influence on recent and past research on unemployment. The model assumes that there exists a market for labour that responds quickly to real-wage variations. With enough wage flexibility it is assumed that market clearing in the labour market will occur. Unemployment, if it arises, is either frictional or voluntary. One way of explaining persistent unemployment within this framework is to assume the presence of institutional changes that impose rigidities on the economic system, preventing the price mechanism from working. Interwar economists, such as Pigou, rationalised the persistence of mass unemployment, relative to the past, in terms of greater wage rigidity introduced by two major institutional changes: first, the rapid spread of unionisation between 1900 and 1920 and, secondly, the introduction of a fairly comprehensive national insurance system between 1911 and 1920.

An alternative way of explaining persistent unemployment within auction market models is to consider the implications of price expectations for unemployment. If the price level cannot be predicted accurately unemployment may result. For example, if economic agents overestimate the price level in the current period, conjectures of the expected value of real variables will be inappropriate to generate market clearing. A high expected price level means that real wages are perceived by workers as being too low which will depress the supply of labour as they search for longer to find the right job at the expected real wage. Real money balances will also be perceived as being lower than they actually are, depressing real expenditure[1]. These search theory models assume a degree of information asymmetry: because employers have full knowledge about the price of the product they are supplying, they are more likely to make accurate price predictions. However, workers have to predict the retail price index, increasing the probability of prediction

---

[1] This is often referred to as the 'Pigou effect'. Pigou argued that consumption is a function of wealth and used real money balances to measure of wealth.

errors. If employers and workers held the same expectations of real wages the effect on unemployment would be small. For such a model to explain persistent unemployment individuals have repeatedly to make the error of overestimating the price level; the individual is not credited with an ability to learn from experience but continues to form expectations adaptively, repeating mistakes from the past.

KEYNESIAN MODELS OF THE LABOUR MARKET

A large number of models have been placed in the general class of 'Keynesian' perspectives. The basic premise underlying all Keynesian models is that the labour market may not clear because insufficient aggregate demand is generated by the macroeconomic system. The model of a demand-constrained unemployment equilibrium can be illustrated using the work of Barro-Grossman (1971). Figure 3.2 illustrates a number of features of these early Keynesian perspectives. The auction market equilibrium (point A) will fail to arise not because institutional rigidities in the labour market have pushed real wages above equilibrium, but because conditions outside the labour market (within a general equilibrium framework, if the goods market does not clear there will be knock-on effects on the labour market), as represented by the line BE_D, have determined a level of effective demand which is lower than that required to generate full employment.[2] Real wages may settle anywhere between B and C but variations in real wages will not generate full employment, even if the real wage settles at the auction market clearing real wage. One important prediction of this model is that the depressed state of the labour market

---

[2] An alternative way of generating the constrained demand for labour is in terms of an insufficient capital stock to employ all the labour force (Malinvaud, 1978). This may arise either because the long-run growth of the capital stock is insufficient given the exogenous growth of the labour force or, in the short run, because depressions lead to falling investment.

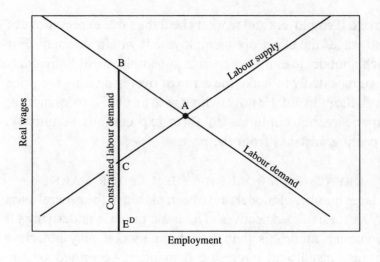

Figure 3.2: Barro–Grossman model of labour demand

may lead to some downward pressure on real wages, until the low employment 'equilibrium' is reached (point C). If this does take place the model predicts that as aggregate demand increases real wages will rise as employment rises – i.e., real wages are expected to follow a pro-cyclical movement with employment. This is in contrast to the market clearing auction market model where real wages are expected to follow a contra-cyclical pattern: only if real wages fall will employment increase.

Although this model can explain some of the features of unemployment and real-wage behaviour, it does so using the *ad hoc* assumption of an *exogenously* given aggregate demand constraint.

IMPLICIT CONTRACTS, EFFICIENCY WAGES AND INSIDER–OUTSIDER MODELS

Recently economists have set themselves the task of explaining unemployment without simply appealing to exogenous explanations. This has led to the development of models that provide more convincing microfoundations for unemployment theory.

Implicit contract theory argues that the labour market should not be viewed as an auction market but as a market in which long-run contractual relationships between buyer and seller predominate. These may take the form of formal employment contracts but more often will be manifested as 'implicit contracts'. In these perspectives the firm is basically acting like an insurance company for the worker, guaranteeing a stable wage path during booms and slumps. The advantages to the firm are observed in the form of better labour relations and more contented (and possibly more productive) workers. The contrast to the ideas of the auction market should be made clear: while in auction market models workers are assumed to push up wages above market clearing, in implicit contract models wage rigidity is the outcome of the firm's profit-maximising strategy.

In efficiency wage models, employers are assumed to find it difficult to monitor work effort and the potential productivity of workers. Since firms cannot easily distinguish between high and low productivity workers, the higher the firm's wage offer the higher the average quality of labour attracted. The wage offer can thus be used as a screening device to increase the pool of high quality labour available to the firm. Another function of a high wage offer by firms is to retain labour and reduce turnover costs. Models of efficiency wages also emphasise the problems of 'moral hazard'; because potential productivity and effort are difficult to monitor, the firm uses the high wage offer to discourage shirking. By offering high wages, the punishment for shirking (i.e., the loss of employment) is increased, thus reducing its occurrence. In such models wages are set at a high level because of the profit-maximising behaviour of firms. Although unemployed workers may try to underbid workers in employment, the firm has no incentive to accept the offer because they do not wish to attract the characteristics that accompany low wages.

In both implicit contract theory and efficiency wage theory market power is assumed to be totally in the hands of firms. A new point of departure introduced by 'insider–outsider' models is to assume that workers have some market power in the wage bargaining process. Because firms find it costly to exchange the current employees (the 'insiders') for unemployed workers (the 'outsiders') an economic rent is generated for insider workers. Involuntary unemployment will thus arise because the wage differentials between insiders and outsiders do not exceed the associated labour turnover costs of the firm. These costs include, *inter alia*, the costs of hiring, firing, training and the non-cooperation of insiders. It is important to realise that unions are not essential to insider–outsider models, although they may act to increase the bargaining power of workers where they do exist.

MODELS OF UNEMPLOYMENT HYSTERESIS: HISTORY-DEPENDENT EQUILIBRIA

One stylised fact that recent unemployment theories have tried to address is the phenomenon of unemployment hysteresis. Over different periods in time unemployment has shown a tendency to persist, rising in steps, and remaining unresponsive to favourable aggregate demand and supply conditions. An example will show clearly what is meant by this phenomenon: following the 1973–9 adverse oil shocks, European unemployment rose sharply in the 1970s and 1980s without any tendency to revert to pre-1973 trends, despite the more favourable conditions in the 1980s relative to the 1970s. A similar pattern was observed in the interwar period: unemployment took a step increase in the 1920s and settled on a higher level relative to the past.

A number of factors have been emphasised to explain this

history-dependent 'equilibrium' path of unemployment. First, it has been noted that, while aggregate demand or supply shocks may generate a short-term rise in unemployment, such unemployment will result in atrophy of human capital. Moreover, in a high unemployment environment it is difficult for reliable and productive workers to signal their qualities by holding jobs, and this reduces demand for their labour. The social psychology literature has also noted the importance of the phenomenon of 'cognitive dissonance' in decision making: once workers have realised that it is more difficult to get back into the labour market than they had originally anticipated, as rationalising agents, they may begin to accept their unemployed state which acts to reduce the extent of job search activity by the unemployed. Thus, the atrophy of skills and loss of market signals is further reinforced by psychological responses from workers.

Secondly, an adverse shock can reduce employment and the capital stock via an adverse effect on the level of investment. Even with more favourable circumstances employment may not rise because the capital stock is not adequate to generate increasing employment: it takes time to rebuild the capital stock to a level that will absorb the labour force.

Thirdly, insider–outsider models can also be used to understand the phenomenon of hysteresis. In the most simple models it has been assumed that 'outsiders' play no role in the wage-bargaining process. Hence, the real wage is determined by a bargaining process between the 'insiders' and employers. In the absence of adverse shocks the level of employment and real wages would have been set at a level that sustains the employment of the insiders. In the presence of adverse shocks that reduce employment, some workers lose their insider status. If the unemployed have no effect on wage bargaining (for the reasons discussed above), unemployment shows no tendency to return to its pre-shock level. The path of unemployment is determined by the history of specific shocks, some of which may be favourable and some adverse.

GROWTH THEORY AND UNEMPLOYMENT

The frameworks we have been considering so far, with the exception of models of hysteresis, are all concerned with explanations of unemployment at a point in time. Further insights can be gained by relating the problems of unemployment to the problems of economic growth and structural change. For example, in the early growth models of Harrod-Domar and Solow a distinction was drawn between the *actual*, *warranted* and *natural* growth* paths. The actual path is that observed historically; the warranted rate can be defined as that path which leaves entrepreneurs satisfied with their intertemporal investment-saving decisions; the natural path is determined by the labour force growth and the rate of (exogenously determined) technological change.

Harrod argued that unemployment results from exogenous demographic and technological influences because equilibrating mechanisms between these growth paths do not exist. One such situation arises if

$$G_n > G_W$$

G_n = rate of growth of the labour force augmented by technological progress (the natural growth rate)
G_W = warranted rate of growth

Thus, demographic trends, which will be partly the result of exogenous socio-demographic influences from the past and international migration behaviour, could be important in determining excess labour supply conditions in the current period. Even if the economy does respond to price signals, as the neoclassical growth model assumes, the adjustment path may be so long that Harrod's analysis is helpful for understanding particular historical epochs.[3]

Economic growth is also associated with long-run structural change. The nature of structural change may generate locational and occupational maldistributions of labour that could result in the phenomenon of structural unemployment. Structural change itself may be the result of long-run tendencies in the economy or the result of specific historical shocks. The regional and occupational distribution of interwar unemployment suggests that there was a serious structural unemployment problem. Unemployment rates were markedly higher in the industrial regions of North England, Wales and Scotland; London and the south-east, the south-west of England and the Midlands fared better. This, in turn, reflected the concentration of the staple export industries (iron and steel, coal, shipbuilding and cotton) in the high unemployment regions. The regions with relatively low unemployment were the centres of car production, distribution and drink production, industries that were growing very rapidly in the interwar years.

SOME EMPIRICAL QUESTIONS

This overview raises a number of empirical questions:

- Did the institutional changes resulting from the introduction of welfare systems lead to a new equilibrium in the interwar period that entailed persistently higher levels of unemployment relative to the past?
- In what ways was aggregate demand a constraint to full employment in this period?
- The step increase in the unemployment rate in the early interwar period suggests the existence of hysteresis effects: to

---

[3] Harrod's framework emphasises long-run capital shortages as an explanation of unemployment. An analogy can be drawn with modern theories of hysteresis which have emphasised capacity shocks as an explanation for the persistence of unemployment.

what extent was this pattern the outcome of transitory shocks having persistent effects?

- How important were exogenous demographic changes in explaining the rise of unemployment?
- Long-run economic growth entails a process of structural change: to what extent was unemployment structural during this period?

MODELS OF MARKET CLEARING

Various strands of the auction market theories have been considered to be relevant to the interwar period. Within these models unemployment will result if real wages are set at too high a level because of specific institutional changes such as the influence of national insurance schemes.

UNEMPLOYMENT AND NATIONAL INSURANCE

Discussions have focused on the idea that maladjustments were introduced into the functioning of the UK labour market by the implementation of national insurance schemes (Benjamin and Kochin, 1979; Beenstock and Warburton, 1984). The unemployment benefit scheme is seen as raising the ratio of unemployment benefits to average wages (often referred to as the 'replacement ratio') which can lead to a rise in unemployment via two identifiable mechanisms. First, the number of workers offering themselves for employment is expected to increase, thus raising the participation ratio of the labour force.[4] This comes about because the relative price changes resulting from the introduction of a national insurance system are expected to

---

[4] The theory distinguishes between those workers who 'offer' themselves for work in order to gain benefits, but who are not actually seeking employment, and those who are genuinely seeking work.

influence the trade-off between leisure and work, increasing the opportunity cost of leisure.[5] Secondly, the existence of a generous national insurance scheme is expected to lead to a reduction in the number of workers *actually* offering themselves for employment: a high replacement ratio implies a subsidy to the activity of search, making people more choosy in the type of employment they seek, leading to a rise in the level of search unemployment. Benjamin and Kochin (1979) argued that the magnitude of these effects on aggregate unemployment was very large:

> We estimate that the insurance system raised the unemployment rate by five to eight percentage points on average and that in the absence of the system, unemployment would have been at normal levels through much of the period.

The main piece of evidence that allowed Benjamin and Kochin to draw this inference was an econometric study of unemployment for the period 1920–38. They estimated the following regression equation (t-values in parenthesis):

$$U_t = 5.9 + 18.3(B/W)_t - 90.0\ (\log Q - \log Q^*)_t + \varepsilon_t \ \ldots (1)$$
$$(2.64)(4.66) \qquad -(8.30)$$

U_t = unemployment level
B/W = benefits–wage ratio
$\log Q - \log Q^*$ = log difference between actual and trend output
ε_t = a random error process

Equation (1) models the *level* of unemployment as being determined by the level of the replacement ratio and the deviations of aggregate output from trend output (to capture aggregate demand effects). A rise in the replacement ratio is expected to raise unemployment; an adverse shock to output

[5] The existence of a national insurance minimum income also creates a lower bound for the real wage, reducing real-wage flexibility.

(such as the cyclical depressions of 1920–1 and 1929–32) is also expected to raise unemployment. Benjamin and Kochin found that although aggregate demand variations had a significant impact on unemployment most of the rise was explained by the level of the benefit–wage ratio. Since the validity of the Benjamin and Kochin conclusion hinges on the econometric soundness of this model, some attention has to be given to their estimation procedures. A number of serious objections have been raised in relation to their methodology. First, the economic interpretation of their results is not clear because it is difficult to identify whether their equation represents a demand function or a supply function for labour: the replacement ratio (B/W) will influence labour supply and the aggregate demand variable ($\log Q - \log Q^*$) will influence labour demand. This gives rise to an 'identification problem'* because their single equation model cannot distinguish demand from supply shifts. Moreover, if, as would be expected, unemployment and wages are determined simultaneously, the single equation model is clearly mis-specified since it assumes only one directional influence from the exogenous variables to the dependent variable – unemployment. Secondly, the econometric validity of the equation depends on the assumption of 'trend-stationarity' in the series being analysed; by this we mean that the series has a stable trend path. Many studies since Benjamin and Kochin have found that unemployment levels are described by the phenomenon of hysteresis (Blanchard and Summers, 1986), invalidating the use of the simple econometric tests specified above. As can be seen from figure 3.1 the unemployment rate rose in a step function pattern during 1919–21.

More disaggregated evidence can be brought to bear on these issues. The Benjamin and Kochin view is best seen as a microeconomic hypothesis. Eichengreen (1987) examines a microeconomic data set of unemployed groups in London found in the 'New Survey of London Life and Labour'. A statistically significant effect of benefits on unemployment is only observed for secondary workers, not household heads, suggesting a much more limited effect than reported by Benjamin and Kochin. Collins (1982) found that when equation (1) is tested using the disaggregated data from twelve sectors the replacement ratio is not statistically significant for nine of those sectors, including the high unemployment sectors of coal, cotton and shipbuilding. Crafts (1987) has shown that the Benjamin and Kochin results do not apply to the long-term unemployed, who formed an increasing proportion of the unemployed in the 1930s. Moreover, in models with more clearly specified labour demand and supply relationships, Hatton (1983) found that the mechanism of influence of the replacement ratio was via employers' hoarding of labour, not the worker's supply of labour; in periods of adverse economic shocks employers are more willing to lay off workers if the replacement ratio is high. For these reasons the Benjamin and Kochin equilibrium explanation for the rise in unemployment has not been accepted by economic historians. However, such a rejection is not sufficient to argue that real-wage problems may not have arisen via other mechanisms.

THE 'WAGE-GAP' AND UNEMPLOYMENT

One idea that has received some attention recently is the wage-gap* that may have arisen in the early post-1918 reconstruction period (Broadberry, 1986). A wage-gap describes a situation where labour productivity growth falls behind the rise in real-wage costs. Dowie (1975) emphasised that the negotiated introduction of the eight-hour day in 1919 resulted in a major inflationary pressure on the UK economy. Average weekly hours fell from 54 to 47, a 13 per cent fall. Since the reduction in hours was made without a reduction in the weekly wage, the *average* rise in real hourly wages amounted to about 13 per cent.

Broadberry (1986) argues that the wage-gap arising from the hours of work change of 1919 induced a *permanent* shift of the supply-side conditions affecting the labour market by creating a situation where the real-wage index remained permanently above the labour productivity index throughout the interwar period, in marked contrast to the more favourable conditions after 1945. To derive this result Broadberry plots the labour productivity index and the weekly real-wage index (see figure 3.3). However, the result of a *persistent* wage-gap is dependent on which price index is used to deflate nominal wages (Thomas 1994a). Since the wage-gap attempts to measure the cost of labour in the light of productivity, the most relevant price index to use for deflating nominal wages is the price index of final output. Such an index is provided by the GDP deflator. Instead, Broadberry deflates by the retail price index. Deflating nominal wages by the GDP deflator (to measure the product real wage) gives very different results for the wage-gap.[6] Figure 3.4 shows that, although a significant wage-gap arose in 1919–20, this is eliminated by 1922. The level of the productivity index lies above the real-wage index throughout 1922–38. The wage-gap is a *transitory* feature of the early post-First World War period, with significant implications for the 1920–1 depression; if we are to explain interwar unemployment in terms of the effects of this shock, the consistent explanation would be to seek hysteresis effects arising from the transitory shocks of 1919–21. Broadberry's emphasis on a permanent supply-side shift in this period is a misleading explanation for

---

[6] The explanation for these different results is that the retail price index is determined by the large and permanent terms of trade* gain that we observe for Britain between 1913 and 1938. The British terms of trade rose from a level of 100 in 1913 to over 140 in 1921. Throughout the interwar period the index remained in the range of 118 to 150. Since the price of imports is relatively cheap throughout the interwar period, real wages made a permanent gain relative to their level in 1913.

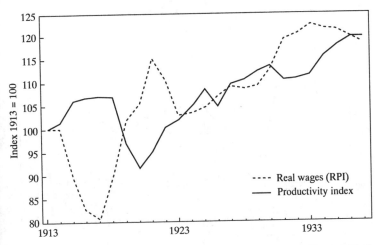

Figure 3.3: Real wages and productivity (real wages deflated by RPI Index)

the rise of mass unemployment during the interwar period.[7]

A further important qualification should also be noted: a wage-gap relates the movement of two endogenous variables in the economic system (real-wage growth and labour productivity growth). Thus, a wage-gap can arise both from changes within the labour market and changes in other markets. To illustrate the relevance of this point consider the following definition of the profit rate (Π/K) which is important in determining the investment, output and productivity path of an economy

$$\frac{\Pi}{K} = \frac{\Pi}{Y} \cdot \frac{Y}{K}$$

[7] The different measures of real wages are expected to influence different decision making processes. For example, the permanent increase of consumer real wages is expected to have a permanent effect on the labour market by resulting in a change in the trade-off between work and leisure, stimulating a rise in the participation ratio of the labour force. However, Hatton (1988) finds that such effects had small impacts on the level of unemployment.

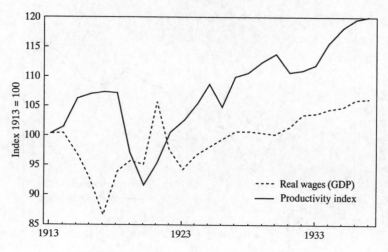

*Figure 3.4: Real wages and productivity
(real wages deflated by GDP deflator)*

Π = profits
Y = income
K = capital stock

The hours of work change in 1919 clearly acted to lower profit shares (Π/Y) and thus, profit rates. Profit shares fell significantly over the trans-war years of 1913–24 (Matthews *et al.*, 1982). To keep a perspective on the relative importance of the shortening of the working week in depressing profitability, however, we also need to consider other factors which influenced profitability during the period. The trans-war years also saw major changes taking place in the capital–output ratio. As can be seen from figure 3.5 the capital–output ratio rose rapidly over the period. This increase over the trans-war period can be further broken down into a rise in the physical capital–output ratio and in the relative price of capital goods. The immediate post-war period created a high demand for capital goods both at home and abroad which pushed up their relative prices, depressing profitability in the capital-using sectors.

In chapter 4 we also show that a number of adverse policy

70

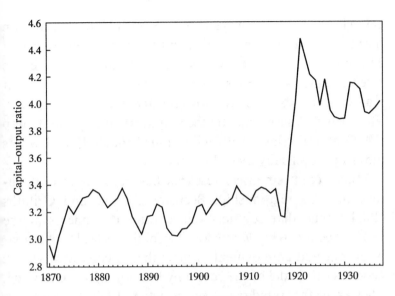

Figure 3.5: Capital–output ratio (1870–1937: current prices)

shocks had the effect of reducing output in the severe depression of 1920–1: first, the appreciated real exchange rate resulted in an import penetration of the domestic market; secondly, the contractionary monetary policy resulted in a permanent increase in the real debt burden. Given the persistence of these effects after 1921 this resulted in a permanent rise in the physical capital–output ratio during the interwar period relative to the period 1870–1913. Thus, it seems clear that a number of forces were generating adverse effects on profitability and investment during the early post-war reconstruction period. To only emphasise the hours of work change of 1919 fails to recognise that a problem that manifests itself within the labour market need not be caused solely, if at all, within the labour market.

KEYNESIAN PERSPECTIVES

Research on the empirical relevance of Keynesian quantity-constrained models for the interwar period has focused on the behaviour of the real-wage employment relationship and on the importance of aggregate demand effects on unemployment. The movement of real wages over the business cycle has received much attention since Keynes (1939) who argued that real wages are expected to move positively with employment. This view was supported by the empirical findings of Dunlop (1938) and Tarshis (1939) who argued that UK real wages moved procyclically over the trade cycle.

Much recent empirical research has been directed at unravelling this relationship. Beenstock, Capie and Griffiths (1984) argue that counter-cyclical wage movements in the 1929–37 period were *fully* responsible for the cyclical fluctuations in output and employment, a view that is consistent with a neoclassical model of the economy but not a Keynesian one. They argue that rapid real-wage growth in 1929–32 resulted in depression and unemployment via a number of demand and supply mechanisms similar to those of Benjamin and Kochin (1979). Moderate real-wage growth from 1932 onwards generated rapid employment growth and a significant output recovery. This monocausal explanation has been significantly qualified by Beenstock and Warburton (1986) who argue that although the counter-cyclical real-wage behaviour was important, it was not the only influence on the UK labour market.

The neoclassical view has been questioned by Dimsdale (1984), Worswick (1984) and Dimsdale, Nickell and Horsewood (1989): their evidence suggests that aggregate demand variations were a more important factor in explaining unemployment variations. Dimsdale (1984) has calculated a variety of measures for real wages for the period 1920–38. Figure 3.6 shows these measures for the manufacturing sector. Real wages (deflated by retail prices) show a persistent upward trend from 1924 to 1935 and do not decline until 1936. Thus, this evidence does not support the contention that the behaviour of real wages changed significantly after 1932.

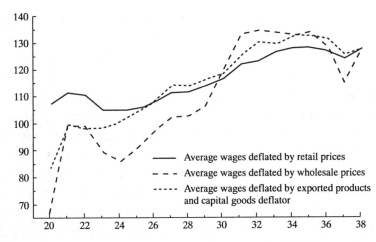

Figure 3.6: Real wages in manufacturing, 1920–38 (1938 prices)
Source: *Dimsdale, 1984, table 1, p. 95.*

In terms of the demand for labour it is necessary to consider the cost of labour to the firm and this requires an indicator of own product real wages. The absence of a suitable price deflator makes it difficult to draw any firm conclusions. One method that has been used in the literature is to deflate wages by wholesale prices. These indices show a rapid increase of real wages between 1929 and 1932 before stabilising between 1932 and 1936. However, the use of the wholesale price index as a deflator is seriously flawed: up to 1930 the index reflected movements in both input and output prices and it is only the latter that is applicable to the measurement of own product real wages. The distortions caused by using this index are particularly severe in the interwar period due to the volatility of raw material prices. In an attempt to overcome this problem Dimsdale calculated own product real wages using a weighted average of export and capital goods prices as one price index and the GDP deflator as another. Both these series rise throughout the recovery and peak during the mid 1930s, suggesting some evidence of procyclical real-wage movements in the early stages of the recovery period.

Another strand of research has been to test for the importance of aggregate demand variations in accounting for unemployment variations. A number of studies have documented the statistical and economic significance of aggregate demand variations (Broadberry, 1983, 1986; Dimsdale, 1984; Hatton, 1988a; Worswick, 1984; Dimsdale, Nickell and Horsewood, 1989). Even those working in a new classical perspective have accepted the relevance of cyclical aggregate demand variables in explaining some phases of interwar unemployment: Benjamin and Kochin (1979) noted the importance of aggregate demand variations in 1920–1 and 1929–32. Similarly Beenstock and Warburton (1986) documented the significance of aggregate demand effects in an econometric model of the interwar economy.

One aspect of the aggregate demand perspective that needs further evaluation is the persistent effects of the adverse aggregate demand shocks of 1919–21. The monetary and exchange rate policies resulted in a persistent output reduction via the effects of an appreciated exchange rate and a rise in the real debt–income ratio of the economy (see chapters 2 and 4). Thus, one way of clarifying the mechanisms by which aggregate demand constraints influence the level of unemployment in this period is to emphasise that adverse transitory demand shocks may have long-term effects on the equilibrium path of the economy.

Given the large output and trade fluctuations of the world economy in this period it would be surprising if aggregate demand variables were not important in explaining some of the features of the unemployment problem. It is important to realise, however, that studies that emphasise the impact of aggregate demand shocks are not advocating a monocausal Keynesian perspective; they support a weaker view that aggregate demand constraints had a role to play within a multicausal framework. Hatton (1988a) concludes that a number of models are consistent with the interwar data; Broadberry (1983, 1986) notes the importance of aggregate demand variations but also puts much weight on the supply-side changes including a wage-gap in the early post-war reconstruction period. Dimsdale *et al.* (1989) note the importance of aggregate demand variations but also emphasise that wage rigidity is essential to understand the dynamics of demand shocks in generating unemployment. As will be seen in our remaining empirical discussions Keynesian perspectives to unemployment may offer relevant insights into the unemployment problem but they are far from offering a complete explanation.

UNEMPLOYMENT HYSTERESIS

The pattern of unemployment rates over the interwar years suggests a *prima facie* case that hysteresis effects were present: following a major transitory shock there was no tendency for the unemployment rate to return to some well-defined pre-war mean value. Looking at unemployment rates over a long-run time period (see figure 3.1) it is quite clear that a significant change occurs in the interwar years. The pre-1913 unemployment series can be described as cyclical and stationary: the unemployment rate rose and fell around a fairly stable average level of 5 per cent. In contrast, unemployment rates in the early interwar years rose in a step-function with no tendency to return to this mean value; instead the unemployment rate settled on a new mean value that was about double the pre-1913 rate (see appendix to this chapter).

How is this process of unemployment persistence to be explained? A number of theoretical perspectives have already been discussed. Economic historians have argued that these perspectives can help us to understand the interwar experience. The human capital perspective has been emphasised in the work of Crafts (1987); he pointed out that the long-term unemployed increased as a proportion of the total unemployed from 5 per cent in the 1920s to 25 per cent in the 1930s. Crafts further showed that the probability of finding employment was dependent on the duration of unemployment: hence, the atrophy of skills and the psychological demoralisation became worse over time as the proportion of the long-term unemployed in total unemployment rose. Insider–outsider models have also been seen as relevant to understanding the path of unemployment. Crafts (1989) found that the responsiveness of wages to the level of long-term unemployment was insignificant, a result that is consistent with insider–outsider models.

A number of inconsistencies in these explanations of unemployment hysteresis should, however, be noted. First, both the human capital and the insider–outsider frameworks are not institutionally specific. Yet unemployment hysteresis is a phenomenon specific to the interwar years and not of the pre-1913 era. Of course some aspects of these models can be made institutionally specific; for example, insider–outsider influences may have been strengthened by rapid development of trade unions during 1900–20. However, union power is on the decline during the interwar years without any significant effect on the persistence of unemployment.[8] Second, these hysteresis mechanisms are more relevant to explain the persistence of unemploynent in the 1930s than in the 1920s. It was in the 1930s that the problem of long-term unemployment is most acute; the duration of the depression of 1929–32 created a group of long-term unemployed who lost human capital and market signals. In the 1920s long-term unemployment accounted for only a small proportion of total unemployment

---

[8] Trade union density fell from 45 per cent of the labour force in 1920, to 36 per cent in 1921 and 26 per cent by 1929.

(Crafts, 1987). However, at the macroeconomic level the persistence channels during the 1930s are weak – the unemployment rate returns to the mean level of the 1920s by 1937. The evidence supports Thomas' (1994b) view that the labour market in the 1930s is bifurcated: economic recovery created a demand for labour that was acting to reduce unemployment rates, while the hysteresis effect of the depression was creating new persistence channels.

The step rise of unemployment in the 1920s is best explained within a different framework to the hysteresis channels observed in the 1930s. The business cycle depression of 1920–1 generated persistent adverse effects on output and employment. First, the hours of work change of 1919 had an adverse supply-side effect on the labour market; secondly, monetary policy during 1919–21 had adverse effects on aggregate output that persisted into the 1920s. Thus, the hysteresis channel is not arising from labour market dynamics, but is instead the outcome of an interaction of policy influences on equilibrium output and employment.

An alternative hypothesis to consider in this context is whether interwar unemployment was predominantly influenced by long-term factors rather than hysteresis effects. Two long-term developments that may have influenced unemployment trends are the disintegration of world trade, and the politically induced reductions in international migration flows. World trade grew at a significantly reduced rate in the interwar years as compared with the pre-1913 period; in the 1930s world trade collapsed even further. Given that much of unemployment was concentrated in the export sectors one may partly explain unemployment persistence in terms of a long-term collapse of world trade leading to a long-term structural collapse of the export sectors. The unemployed were heavily concentrated in the staple sectors* of coal, shipbuilding, engineering, cotton and iron and steel. Secondly, migration restrictions from the

New World, symbolised by the American Immigration Act of 1924, meant that the UK labour market could no longer adjust to adverse shocks with mass migration[9] (as was the case in the 1880s and 1900s). Instead, mass emigration gave way to mass unemployment.

The evidence considered suggests that hysteresis effects were present in the interwar period, particularly in the 1930s. However, unemployment persistence was reinforced by the effects of adverse long-term shocks on the UK economy and changes in the international adjustment mechanisms (such as migration flows).

DEMOGRAPHIC CHANGES AND UNEMPLOYMENT

We noted above that autonomous demographic trends could influence the equilibrium in the labour market: if labour force growth is in excess of warranted economic growth unemployment will result. It can be shown that demographic trends helped to generate excess supply in the labour market during this period. The proportion of the population of working age (excluding the young and the old) increased from 64 per cent in the pre-1913 period to 70 per cent in the interwar period: during 1924–37, while population growth was 0.4 per cent per annum, labour force growth was 1.5 per cent per annum. Two other complications further reinforced these adverse supply conditions. During 1911–38 all the increase in population lay in the over forty-five age group; the proportion of those under forty-five actually fell slightly. Such a demographic structure reduced labour mobility, since the age group between twenty-five and forty-four is the most mobile.

[9] During 1870–1913 the mean level of international migration from the UK as a percentage of the labour force was 1.5 per cent; during 1925–38 this ratio fell to 0.4 per cent. In fact, during the 1930s the inflow of migrants into the UK was greater than the outflow.

Although many of these demographic changes can be described as having long-term origins, or as being induced by exogenous international influences, we cannot assume that all the observed growth in labour supply was autonomous. Beenstock and Warburton (1986) and Matthews (1986) have pointed out that interwar labour supply was responsive to real-wage trends. Thus, as real wages rose on trend during 1924–37 this generated supply-side effects that compounded the unemployment problem. However, using quarterly data for the interwar period Hatton (1988a) found that although these supply responses were statistically significant, they were small in magnitude: the adverse supply conditions can best be viewed as a result of long-term demographic trends and international policy changes.

STRUCTURAL UNEMPLOYMENT

Structural unemployment refers to the *locational* and *occupational* characteristics of unemployment. Given the high rates of unemployment in the industrial north and in the slow growing staple sectors, much of interwar unemployment can be described as structural in nature. Glynn and Booth (1983) have gone as far as to argue that 60 to 80 per cent of UK unemployment can best be thought of as structural in nature. Keynes came to a similar conclusion in an article in *The Times* in 1937:

> I believe that we are approaching, or have reached, the point where there is not much advantage in applying a further general stimulus at the centre. So long as surplus resources were widely diffused between industries and localities it was no great matter at what point in the economic structure the impulse of an increased demand was applied. But the evidence grows that the economic structure is unfortunately rigid.

Care needs to be taken when evaluating such views. Glynn and Booth's estimate is based on a view that unemployment can be decomposed into three component parts: frictional, cyclical and structural. Thus, all the differential in regional and occupational unemployment rates has been described by them as structural. However, structural unemployment is not independent of the level of economic activity: a severe depression increases the degree of structural unemployment and a boom acts to reduce it. Hatton (1986) has shown that internal migration is influenced by the level of aggregate economic activity; hence a higher level of overall activity would have acted to reduce regional unemployment. Internal migration rates were significantly higher between 1925 and 1931 than between 1931 and 1936, falling by about a third.

Another reason why the conventional classification is inappropriate is that the level of structural unemployment was partly determined by the macroeconomic policy regime. In the 1920s, the policy of returning to the gold standard at the pre-1913 parity resulted in an overvaluation of the real exchange rate in 1920–2 (Broadberry, 1986) – an overvaluation that persisted (at a lower level) well into the 1920s. Broadberry (1984) has also noted that a structural unemployment problem was observed in all the overvalued currencies of the 1920s, including UK, Denmark, Norway and Sweden. Thus, a more appropriate exchange rate policy in the 1920s would have significantly lowered so-called structural unemployment.

Finally, to the extent that hysteresis effects were present, via human capital and insider–outsider effects, these should be distinguished from a structural problem. Much of the long-term unemployment problem was focused on the staple export sectors; to this extent the problem can be labelled as structural. However, given that hysteresis effects explain some of the unemployment in these sectors (Crafts, 1987) the policy options would be quite different to those that can be used to solve structural unemployment. The state should have followed a policy of rebuilding human capital or 'enfranchising' the outsiders by increasing the demand for labour, not pursuing an expansionist regional policy (Lindbeck, 1993).

CONCLUSIONS

- This survey suggests that the simple generalisations of static macroeconomic models are inadequate to help us understand the new phenomenon of mass unemployment: interwar unemployment cannot be explained either by the simple neoclassical auction market models or the simple Keynesian aggregate demand deficiency models.

- Neo-classical perspectives that have emphasised the role of the benefit system to explain the high unemployment rates of this period are not convincing. Even if benefit systems have an effect on the level of unemployment, the severity of the interwar unemployment problem cannot be explained within this framework.

- The relative price distortions of the immediate post-First World War period, in the goods and the labour market, depressed profitability, investment and capacity. Although this was a transitory feature it had significant implications for the amplitude of the 1920–1 depression.

- Hysteresis effects are observed in the path of unemployment, with the development of long-term unemployment in the 1930s. However, at the aggregate level other shocks were compensating for the new hysteresis channels of the 1930s, leading to a total unemployment rate in 1937 that was comparable to that observed in the 1920s. The hysteresis effects of the shocks of the early 1920s are not so clear; to the extent that they are present they are not working via simple labour market dynamics, such as the creation of long-term unemployment.

- Since the economy was influenced both by short-term shocks (such as the wage-gap of 1919–20) and long-term changes

81

(such as the disintegration of world trade and the collapse of international migration flows), it is sensible to conclude that a combination of permanent and transitory shocks determined the step rise of unemployment in the 1920s relative to the pre-1913 period.

- Demographic trends were adverse, given the level of aggregate demand and other unfavourable shocks in the 1920s and 1930s. However, even if a component of the labour force growth rate can be seen as exogenous this can only explain a small part of aggregate unemployment.

- The perspective of categorising unemployment into a number of clearly labelled boxes (e.g., structural, cyclical and frictional) is misleading and of limited use for policy analysis. The different types of unemployment are interrelated and the complexity of these relationships are compounded by the phenomenon of hysteresis.

APPENDIX   UNEMPLOYMENT DATA

The estimate of unemployment levels before 1914 was derived from the trade union records by the Ministry of Labour (Pigou, 1927). Feinstein (1972) has pointed out a number of serious defects as a representation of the rate of unemployment for the labour force as a whole. The series covers a very small proportion of the industrial labour force, with a clear overrepresentation of engineering, shipbuilding and the metal trades. These industries accounted for three fifths of union membership in the 1870s and 1880s and two fifths in the 1890s; moreover, within these industries the sample selection covers only trade unionists who were skilled workers during this period. The disaggregated evidence suggests that the forces generating business cycle fluctuations in engineering, shipbuilding and the metal trades (which accounted for about 10 per cent of total industrial output) were quite different from many other sectors. For example, fluctuations in agricultural output (which still accounted for over 15 per cent of GDP in the 1870s) were distinctly different from these three industries; coal production (which accounted for 18 per cent of the industrial production index) was different yet again. Thus, generalisations about unemployment trends before 1914 should be made with care.

For the interwar period the reliability of information on unemployment is significantly better. Unemployment insurance, which was first introduced in 1911, covered 60 per cent of all employees in the 1920s, giving us far more representative information on unemployment than the trade union records. The rate of unemployment from the insurance data is calculated as the ratio of those registered as unemployed to the total number insured by the scheme. The average unemployment rate calculated in this way for the period 1921–38 was 14.2 per cent.

It is recognised, however, that the insured occupations averaged higher unemployment levels than the uninsured (such as white-collar workers and domestic servants). Feinstein (1972) calculated unemployment rates for the working population as a whole using information from the Census of Population in 1931. As expected, the total unemployment rate is significantly lower than the insured unemployment rate for the same year. Feinstein corrects for the bias in the *level* of the insurance unemployment rate by adjusting the time-series data for the proportional relationship between the insured and total unemployment rates for 1931 (assuming that the same proportion holds for the other interwar years). During 1921–38 the total unemployment rate averaged 10.9 per cent.

Quite clearly comparisons between pre-1913 and interwar data are difficult to make. However, there is little doubt that the unemployment problem in the interwar period was very much worse. Beveridge (1944) argued that the magnitude of interwar unemployment was *two* to *three* times worse than the prewar level. Even if we accept the lower bound there was a significant rise in unemployment relative to the past.

SELECTED FURTHER READING

Benjamin, D. K. and Kochin, L. A. (1979), 'Searching for an explanation of unemployment in interwar Britain', *Journal of Political Economy*.

Broadberry, S. N. (1986) *The British Economy Between the Wars*, Part III.

Crafts, N. F. R. (1987), 'Long-Term Unemployment in Britain in the 1930s', *Economic History Review*.

Eichengreen, B. and Hatton, T.J. (eds.) (1988), *Interwar Unemployment in International Perspective* (chapter 1).

Hatton, T. J. (1994). 'Unemployment and the Labour Market in Interwar Britain', in Floud, R. and McCloskey, D. N. *The Economic History of Britain Since 1700*, second edition.

CHAPTER 4

ECONOMIC FLUCTUATIONS, 1919–38

INTRODUCTION

During 1919–38 both the UK and the world economy witnessed economic fluctuations that were, in many ways, distinctly different from those of the past. Although business cycles are a recurrent phenomenon their characteristics evolve over time and reflect *inter alia*, the nature of specific shocks, changing policy regimes and other evolutionary changes in the structure of the economy. This chapter describes and explains the cyclical process of the interwar era and in doing so also addresses the issue of why the nature of business cycles changed in the interwar period relative to the past. The macroeconomic data that are analysed are the balanced national accounts of Solomou and Weale (1993) which represent an improvement on previous UK macroeconomic data for the interwar period (for a description of the data see appendix 1 to this chapter).

DESCRIBING BUSINESS CYCLES

Figures 4.1 and 4.2 plot the annual growth rate of GDP and manufacturing output respectively: major depressions can be observed in 1920–1, 1925–6, 1929–32 and less severe downturns in 1927–38 and 1937–8. Figure 4.3 plots the path of gross

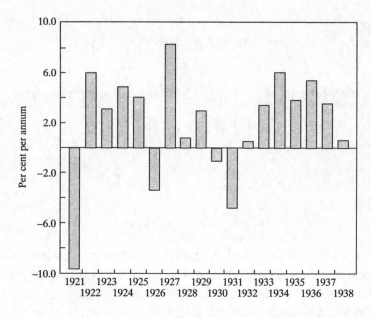

Figure 4.1: Annual growth of GDP, 1921–38

domestic product during the period 1870–1938: a further business cycle feature which needs to be emphasised is that, following the cyclical depression of 1921, the economy failed to return to the previous long-run path. The business cycle shocks of 1919–21 generated a *persistent* adverse output effect, making the analysis of economic growth and business cycles difficult to distinguish. Why this output persistence arose is a question which needs to be addressed if we are to gain an understanding of the full implications of interwar business cycles.

THE CHANGING NATURE OF BUSINESS CYCLES

The traditional interpretation of interwar business cycles is that the UK economy peaked in 1920, 1929 and 1937 yielding a cycle with an average peak to peak duration of 8.5 years

86

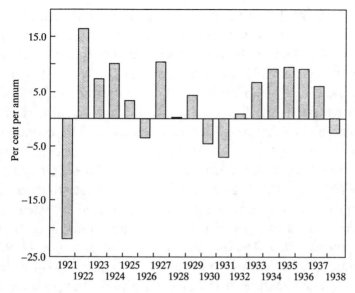

Figure 4.2: Growth of manufacturing, 1921–38

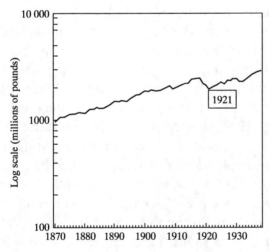

Figure 4.3: Gross domestic product (constant 1900 prices)

(Aldcroft and Fearon, 1969). This is often considered to be comparable to the cycle duration of the pre-1914 era when the Juglar cycle* of eight to nine years punctuated steady long-run economic growth. This interpretation can, however, be questioned on three major counts: first, by neglecting the 1926 and 1928 recessions there is a data selection bias towards seeing regular eight-year cycles where none exist. The economic fluctuations of the 1920s are irregular in amplitude* and duration. Secondly, the idea that the pre-1914 economy was dominated by the Juglar cycle is one that lacks empirical support: the pre-war economy was influenced by irregular cyclical variations, some short term and some long term (Matthews, 1959; Hicks, 1982; Catao and Solomou, 1993; Solomou, 1994). The major continuity with the pre-1914 cycles is the general feature of irregularity. Finally, the persistence resulting from the shocks of 1919–21 further negates the idea of continuity with the cyclical structure of the past: the path of the macroeconomy was permanently displaced by the historical events of the early post-1918 period.

Two important changes in the nature of interwar business cycles stand out: first, the long 'Kuznets swings'* (averaging twenty years in duration) in the level of investment that had influenced the pre-1914 economy were no longer observed. Figures 1A.6 and 4.4 plot gross capital formation over the period 1870–1938: the long swings in investment observed before 1914 gave way to a shorter cycle during 1920–38. Secondly the amplitude of the cycle (measured by the standard deviation of GDP growth) was significantly higher in the interwar than in the pre-1914 era. This is a general feature of the world economy during this period: Table 4.1 shows that most of the major industrial countries saw an increase in macroeconomic volatility in the interwar epoch relative to the past (Sheffrin, 1988; Backus and Kehoe, 1992). A question which we shall return to is: was this increased volatility the

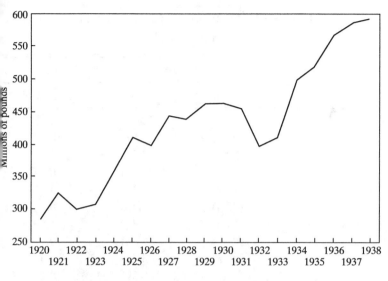

Figure 4.4: Investment levels, 1920–38 (Constant Prices)

result of changes in the underlying endogenous behaviour of the economic system or does it reflect the greater severity of shocks in the interwar period when compared to the pre-1913 era?

CAUSAL FRAMEWORKS

The causal frameworks for modelling business cycle behaviour can be placed into two broad categories: the *propagation* and *impulse* perspectives. The former sees cycles as arising from the endogenous workings of the economic system. The impulse perspective, on the other hand, views cycles as arising from exogenous shocks to the economy. It is worth noting that even random shocks are capable of generating cycles because each shock imposes an adjustment path on the economic system (Slutsky, 1937). Shocks may be due, *inter alia*, to technological change, climatic variability or policy changes. These two approaches to business cycles are not mutually exclusive. For example, a propagation mechanism is needed to convert

89

Table 4.1. Standard deviations of GDP (standard errors in parentheses)

Country	Standard deviations (percentages)		
	Prewar	Inter-war	Post-war
Germany	3.35	10.19	2.30
	(0.32)	(1.61)	(0.28)
Italy	2.52	3.59	2.05
	(0.24)	(0.46)	(0.17)
Japan	2.42	3.13	3.11
	(0.24)	(0.44)	(0.32)
Norway	1.85	3.49	1.76
	(0.16)	(0.65)	(0.17)
Sweden	2.43	3.74	1.45
	(0.37)	(0.59)	(0.12)
United Kingdom	2.12	3.47	1.62
	(0.24)	(0.37)	(0.21)
United States	4.28	9.33	2.26
	(0.38)	(1.27)	(0.18)

Source: Backus and Kehoe (1992).

random shocks into business cycles: without a propagation mechanism a random shock will have random effects, leading to variability in the economy but not cycles of upswings and downswings. Similarly, economists who emphasise the propagation perspective recognise that shocks determine the specific historical details of particular cycles and, thus, can account for why one cycle may be longer than another or why one depression is more severe than another. Partly because of this interaction of causal frameworks it has proved extremely difficult to determine whether economic cycles are best explained by emphasising a propagation or impulse framework.

The recent theoretical literature in this area has focused on two main impulse perspectives: the monetary theory of business cycles and the real business cycle perspective (see Appendix 2 of this chapter). The monetary theory of business cycles explains economic fluctuations as the outcome of discretionary monetary policy changes. Within the rational expectations literature monetary policy has real effects as long as the government is able to introduce an element of surprise, making the policy random or unanticipated. An inflationary monetary shock may have real effects because individuals fail to recognise an absolute price change, confusing it with a relative price change. In Keynesian models monetary shocks will have real effects because the economic system operates with a degree of price and wage rigidity: given nominal wage rigidity, governments can stimulate (depress) the economy with expansionary (contractionary) monetary policy.

Real business cycle (RBC) theory, on the other hand, sees business cycles as resulting from real shocks that shift the supply-side conditions of the economy. For example, a favourable technological shock will lead to cyclical effects on the economy as investment and consumption are stimulated. The extent and nature of the stimulus will depend on whether the shock is perceived to be permanent or transitory.

As a reflection of the existing historical research my focus in this chapter will be on the impulse perspective, documenting the kind of shocks that influenced interwar business cycle behaviour. In following this perspective I am not dismissing the relevance of endogenous economic processes, such as multiplier–accelerator interactions and endogenous expectations induced cycles. However, most of the research in this area has been of a theoretical nature, showing the *possibility* of endogenous economic cycles, without historical or empirical application. Moreover, as noted above an understanding of specific impulses is essential to capture the specific features of particular periods.

In the light of this overview and the description of some of

THEMES IN MACROECONOMIC HISTORY

the key features of interwar business cycles we can pose a number of questions:

- Were business cycle fluctuations due to real or monetary shocks? This question is particularly interesting in the light of the extensive evidence on the post-war and the pre-1913 periods showing that monetary shocks have played a minor role in business cycle fluctuations. The interwar period represents a period of flexible and devalued exchange rates, implying a degree of monetary policy discretion, giving us a 'control' period for comparison with the fixed exchange rate epochs of the classical gold standard (1879–1914) and Bretton Woods (1944–72).
- Why were some short-term business cycle shocks (such as the depression of 1920–1) persistent in their effects? Did this arise from transitory shocks (which had persistent effects on output) or from permanent shocks.
- Why was the amplitude of interwar business cycles so much greater than in the pre-war era? In particular is this feature to be explained by the nature of shocks or by endogenous economic processes.
- Why did the interwar witness 'the passing of the Kuznets swing' (Abramovitz, 1968)?

As a preliminary step in evaluating these questions I will consider the causes of the cyclical depressions of 1921, 1926, 1928, 1930–2 and 1938. This will give us an insight into the kind of impulses generating interwar fluctuations.

INTERWAR DEPRESSIONS

1920–1

This was the most severe slump experienced by the UK economy since the nineteenth century, being more severe in its effects than the world depression of 1929–32. The severity of the depression was also unmatched at the time by that of any other country. In order to understand the recessionary forces of 1920 we have to consider the inflationary path of the immediate post-First World War period: the reconstruction period* generated both demand pull and cost push inflationary pressures. Between 1918 and 1920, the economy operated at full employment, with a rapid growth of demand for consumer and investment goods at home and abroad: this generated demand pull inflationary pressures. Cost push pressures were also present. Dowie (1975) notes the importance of the (negotiated) introduction of the eight-hour day in 1919 as a major inflationary force. The combined effects of demand and cost pressures on the UK inflation rate caused it to rise faster than the US rate.

In November 1919 the government announced the official policy intention of returning to the gold standard at the pre-1913 gold parity. Given the differential between the UK and the US price levels that had arisen between 1913 and 1919, the government was clearly announcing a forthcoming contractionary monetary policy stance. In this period of flexible exchange rates (1919–25) the effect of the restrictive monetary policy announcement was to appreciate the real effective exchange rate (Broadberry, 1986). The restrictive monetary policy also encouraged consumers to hold to inelastic inflationary expectations,[1] reducing consumption and increasing money demand. This implies that the rise in interest rates in April 1920 was not the impulse that pushed the economy into depression but a symbol that recessionary forces had been under way probably from late 1919, resulting from the deflationary monetary policy announcements and the wage-gap* in the labour market (see chapter 3).

One of the outstanding features of the depression of 1921 is

---

[1] The elasticity of price expectations can be defined as the percentage change in the *expected* price level divided by the percentage change in the *actual* price level.

the exceptionally large fall in exports. However, in the light of the circumstances the export collapse cannot be seen as an exogenous shock, accounting for the amplitude of the depression: under flexible exchange rates, the contractionary monetary policy and the supply-side changes in the labour market (arising from the eight-hour day) resulted in an appreciation of the real exchange rate, leading to a large fall in exports. Thus, the collapse of exports, though important for understanding the dynamics of the depression, was not the *cause* in a simple exogenous sense, but a direct result of the contractionary monetary policy measures and supply-side shocks of 1919–21.

1925–6

The 1926 depression is attributable to the effects of the General Strike of the same year. Mining output fell by 44 per cent and exports of goods by 12 per cent. Such a large fall in exports was not related to a world aggregate demand constraint since the world economy was in a strong recovery phase, despite a German depression. Moreover, the bilateral trade and capital flows between Germany and the UK were weak in this period. As a sign of the expanding world trade and income, the export of UK services increased by 15.8 per cent in 1926. It is important to recognise the balance of payments repercussions of this supply shock: imports continued to rise by 4.5 per cent in 1926 relative to 1925 reflecting the short-term nature of the shock. Under the fixed exchange rate regime (1925–31) real interest rates rose, depressing investment and stockbuilding. The very short-term nature of this depression is also reflected in the exceptional speed and strength of the recovery in 1927.

1928–32

The balanced estimate of GDP shows that 1928 is a year of recession in the UK economy (Solomou and Weale, 1993). The contemporary Board of Trade quarterly industrial production

94

indicator shows that a contractionary movement was observed in every quarter in 1928 (see figure 4.5), and there is no evidence that this was induced by a specific short-term event, as in 1926. In the light of this evidence the depression of the late 1920s was a double phased depression with troughs in 1928 and 1932. The accepted interpretation of the depression is that in 1929 UK exports fell significantly, as a result of depression in primary-producing* economies, which acted as an exogenous impulse that pushed the UK economy into depression (Corner, 1956). The UK was, however, manifesting recessionary forces well before the export collapse of 1929. Solomou and Weale (1993) have shown that a combination of external and internal factors were responsible for recession in 1928. Corner is correct to argue that the export of goods saw a major fall in 1929 while they rose by 2 per cent in 1928. However, a different picture emerges when we also consider trade in services. The export of services fell by 7.3 per cent in 1928 leading to overall stagnation in the export of goods and services. Hence, already by 1928 the large fall in American overseas investment was imposing a balance of payments constraint on many primary-producing economies, constraining their purchases of traded services. Given that the UK conducted 40 per cent of its trade with low-income primary-producing countries, this shock to the world economy was rapidly transmitted to the domestic economy.

The downturn of 1928 also had strong domestic origins, characterised by a large fall in investment in dwellings and other buildings and a 22 per cent fall in construction output. The high real interest rates of the late 1920s, associated with an overvalued exchange rate were depressing construction which is recognised as being an interest sensitive sector: Broadberry (1986) estimated that investment in housing during the interwar period had a short-run interest elasticity of -0.55 (i.e., a one percentage point rise in interest rates lowered housing investment

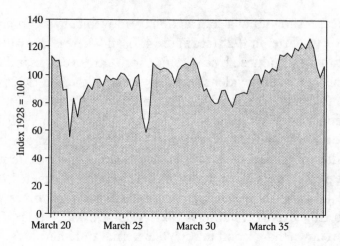

Figure 4.5: Industrial production (quarterly: March 1920 – December 1938)

by half of 1 per cent). The poor performance of the UK non-tradable sector was the main reason for recession in 1928. It is clear that the exchange rate regime adopted in 1925 was not able to sustain stable economic growth. The second shock pushing the economy into recession came in 1929 when exports of goods and services fell significantly: between 1929 and 1931 a reduction of exports was the main depressing shock on UK aggregate demand. Given the regime of fixed exchange rates, the collapse of world income, and in particular the collapse of incomes in primary-producing countries, was a major adverse shock to the UK economy. Monetary shocks were unimportant in explaining the 1929 turning point: both M1 and M2 rose by 3 per cent and 5 per cent respectively during 1929–30 (Capie and Weber, 1985; Capie and Wood, 1994). This does not mean that monetary influences can be dismissed as being unimportant throughout the 1929–32 depression: a useful perspective for modelling the role of money during this period is Hick's idea of a two phase schema of depression: real causes (such as the export contraction) which drove the economy into depression were, with time, compounded by financial and monetary repercussions. These financial and monetary effects were clearly present in 1931 when international financial crises led to rising real interest rates and monetary restraint as the government raised interest rates in an attempt to maintain the value of sterling. Thus, monetary factors are important in explaining the amplitude of the depression, but not the turning point or the early stages of the downswing.

1937–8

The recession of 1937–8 was caused by an 11 per cent contraction in exports. This large fall of exports, however, only induced a mild aggregate recession: GDP grew at 0.7 per cent during 1937–8 compared to a 2 per cent trend growth rate during 1929–37. The mildness of this recession is partly due to the continued rapid rise of government expenditure as the rearmament drive gained momentum from 1935 onwards (Middleton, 1981). Moreover, as the recovery progressed during 1932–7, the role of the export sector in the performance of the macroeconomy diminished; economic growth was increasingly domestically generated as the openness of the economy fell. Hence, the export shock of 1937–8 was less destabilising in this depression than in previous interwar depressions. A further feature explaining the mildness of the 1938 depression is to be found in the new international economic order that was emerging in the 1930s (Eichengreen, 1992). As countries left the gold standard in the 1930s, the national pressures for contractionary fiscal and monetary policies to sustain the gold standard exchange rates were not present to the same extent as in 1929–33. Thus, the international repercussion effects of a large export contraction were much weaker in 1937–8 compared to 1929–33.

REAL OR MONETARY IMPULSES?

This overview allows us to address the question of causality. Quite clearly it is not possible to make a simple or general statement that interwar recessions were due to a series of monetary shocks as would be predicted from a monetary business cycle model. However, monetary policy was influential during particular episodes within this period: for example, during 1920–1 and 1931–2. Monetary policy was also important in the recovery phases of the 1920s and the 1930s (see chapters 2 and 5).

Real shocks also seem to be important impulses in the generation of interwar business cycles. A variety of real shocks impacted on the economic system: the hours of work change of 1919, the General Strike of 1926 and the export contractions of 1928, 1929–31 and 1937–8. It is more difficult to find evidence of *autonomous* technological shocks of the type that the real business cycle literature has emphasised. Within the class of real shocks we can distinguish further between real supply-side shocks (such as the fall in hours of work in 1919) and real demand-side shocks (such as the export shocks of 1929–31 and 1937–8).

The exchange rate regime also helps to define the business cycle features of this period. Splitting the interwar era into three exchange rate regimes, floating (1919–25), fixed (1925–31) and managed (1931–8), the evidence suggests that monetary shocks had their greatest impact in the period of floating. This is of course a simple generalisation since we have only focused on an analysis of the depression years. For a more complete picture we also need to consider the role of money and real factors in the recovery periods (see chapters 2 and 5). However, the result does have some intuitive appeal since we would expect exchange rate flexibility to give a more discretionary policy stance to monetary policy while the gold standard rules of 1925–31 imposed less discretion on the overall policy regime.

THE PERSISTENCE OF OUTPUT SHOCKS

An interesting result of the recent macroeconomics literature is that the path of twentieth century aggregate output has followed a 'random walk': major shocks have resulted in a permanent shift of the equilibrium of the economic system, making it difficult to distinguish between transitory cyclical phenomena and more persistent longer run changes.

Figure 4.3 illustrates the persistent nature of the 1919–21 shocks on GDP. During 1870–1914 GDP followed a steady growth path. The shocks of 1919–21 which have been seen as cyclical in nature in fact had a persistent effect on the interwar economy, with no discernible tendency to return to the original path. In this sense the cyclical shocks of 1919–21 had persistent effects. A number of frameworks can help us understand this random walk in output:

(i) A real business cycle explanation
The models of real business cycles (see appendix 2) are a specific attempt to model this kind of behaviour. If we view technology in a broad Schumpeterian perspective, which includes institutional and organisational changes, there are a number of aspects of the immediate post-First World War reconstruction period that generated adverse effects on output. The institutional change resulting from the fall in hours of work in 1919 acted to shift the production function inwards. Although much of the literature has argued that this generated a persistent adverse effect because the change generated a persistent wage-gap* throughout the interwar period, the evidence for this is not convincing (see chapter 3). The hours of work shock of 1919 generated a wage-gap only during 1919–21.

(ii) Exchange rates and persistence

The policy announcements of 1919 and the contractionary monetary policy stance that was pursued to return the UK to the pre-1913 gold standard parity resulted in an overvaluation of the real exchange rate in 1920–1 (see chapter 2) which compounded the severity of depression relative to other industrial countries. The effect of this was to increase the penetration of foreign suppliers into the UK market making it more difficult for domestic industries to compete even in the more normal period of 1922–9, when the exchange rate overvaluation is significantly reduced. Imports as a proportion of GDP rose from 20 per cent in 1920–1 to 24 per cent in 1922–5. Such a permanent rise in import penetration is consistent with a permanent adverse effect on the *level* of GDP[2].

(iii) Prices and real debt problems

In the early reconstruction period, private debt increased significantly in the expectation of a speedy recovery. The military defeat of Germany led to market euphoria stimulating investment in the staple industries. However, with the deflationary policies of 1919–21 this debt had to be repaid at a significantly reduced price level, increasing the outstanding real debt burden and preventing the growth of new debt to finance investment projects (see chapter 2). Since the price level was forced down permanently by policy measures (as long as the UK remained committed to the gold standard), the level of real indebtedness rose on a permanent basis.

BUSINESS CYCLE VOLATILITY

Macroeconomic fluctuations during the interwar period were of a significantly higher amplitude than those observed in the

---

[2] In the simplest income–expenditure models equilibrium income depends on the multiplier, which is inversely dependent on the savings propensity and the import propensity.

pre-1914 era (see table 4.1). Such evidence raises a number of issues about the structure of interwar economies relative to the past: was the increased volatility due to the increased severity of shocks or to the endogenous workings of the economic system? For example, did the institutional changes of the twentieth century, such as the development of oligopolistic market structures, mass unionisation and welfare systems, necessitate greater quantity adjustments by limiting price flexibility?

Pinpointing the causes of this increased volatility is not an easy task. A number of features are, however, noteworthy. First, increased volatility is very much an international phenomenon. Kindleberger (1983) has attributed this to the leadership structure of the world economy after the First World War: while the USA had made the transition to becoming the major world economic power she did not have the willingness to lead. The share of America in world production rose significantly throughout 1870–1914 and the First World War accelerated this trend. Moreover, the financing of the war by the European countries, in part by borrowing, strengthened America's position as a capital exporter. The American economy was subject to more volatility than the UK, because of the size of primary sectors in its production structure and the more fragile financial institutions. By 1929 America accounted for over 30 per cent of world industrial production[3]: the relatively higher volatility of the American economy was thus easily transmitted to the world economy.

Secondly, increased volatility arose from the exchange rate volatility of the interwar period. The gold standard era of 1870–1914 had seen mild real and nominal exchange rate variations compared to the excessive volatility of 1919–25 and the discrete variations associated with devaluation in 1931 and the managed currency of the 1930s. A correlation seems clear:

---

[3] The League of Nations index of world industrial production gives the US a weight of 31.1 per cent while the UK has a weight of 12.9 per cent.

the amplitude of the business cycle was lower under the more rules-driven international payments system of the pre-First World War gold standard than in the more discretionary policy periods of flexible and devalued exchange rates.[4] The mechanisms by which this correlation can be interpreted as causal can be seen clearly in the above analysis of the impact of the 1919–21 monetary and exchange rate shocks. However, we should also be aware of the problem of reverse causality: it may be because of an increase in underlying instability that nations were forced to adopt flexible and more discretionary exchange rate systems. Moreover, most of the instability of the world economy actually occurred between 1928–31 while countries were on the gold standard. Such evidence has directed much of the recent literature (Temin, 1989; Bernanke and James, 1991; Eichengreen, 1992) to argue that the instabilities of the era were mainly caused by the inappropriateness of returning to the gold standard at the pre-1913 gold parity which gave rise to policy regimes that amplified shocks in the world economic system. The fixed exchange rate of 1925–31, and the macroeconomic policies pursued to achieve and sustain these rates during the 1920s led to amplified downswings. Once countries followed new policy regimes in the 1930s, business cycle volatility was sustained as countries that instituted policy regime changes saw fast cyclical recoveries in the 1930s (Temin, 1989). Thus, the increased business cycle volatility of the interwar period was linked to the exchange rate regime but not in a simple linear manner.

'THE PASSING OF THE KUZNETS SWING'

The pre-1913 UK economy had witnessed irregular Kuznets swings in a number of key variables, including investment,

[4] It should be noted that some discretion was being exercised by Central Banks during the classical gold standard era (Eichengreen, 1992).

consumption, migration, money supply and the balance of trade (Solomou, 1987; Rowthorn and Solomou, 1991). During the interwar era this cyclical adjustment path came to an abrupt end. A number of important institutional changes lie at the heart of this transition.

First, the adjustment mechanisms to cyclical shocks were quite different in the interwar period, relative to the pre-1913 era. For example, while severe depressions before 1913 gave rise to migration waves, legislative changes in the New World (symbolised by the US Immigration Act of 1924) prevented mass emigration.[5] There is much evidence to suggest that migration waves before 1914 were a key variable to the swings in investment and output (Thomas, 1973; Solomou, 1987).

Secondly, the working of the gold standard policy regime of the pre-1913 era meant that adjustment to shocks had to arise via the price mechanism rather than policy regime changes. The institution of the gold standard limited the extent of monetary policy discretion; a laissez-faire attitude to the role of government also limited discretionary fiscal policy; and a unilateral free trade policy prevented the use of trade policy to influence the macroeconomy. The price mechanism did provide some slow adjustment to shocks. For example, depression phases were correlated with a depreciated real exchange rate which stimulated net exports (Solomou and Catao, 1994); this is particularly clear during 1890–1913. In contrast, during the interwar period more policy discretion was observed: governments were using policy discretion in an attempt to return to the gold standard in the early 1920s and in responding to the depression of the 1930s. Such policy discretion introduced new shocks and new adjustment paths during the interwar period relative to the past.

Finally, another factor in the long swing fluctuations of the

[5] Migration as a percentage of total labour force averaged 1.4 per cent during 1870–1913 and 0.3 per cent during 1925–38.

pre-1913 era was an independent agricultural long swing (Solomou, 1987; 1994). Structural change in the economy gave rise to a rapid decline in the size of the agricultural sector during 1870–1913. This meant that swings in agricultural output and productivity had their largest impact during 1870–1890. By the interwar period agricultural fluctuations were not central to macroeconomic fluctuations.

CONCLUSIONS

- The key features of economic fluctuations during the interwar period were quite different from those of the past: both the amplitude and average period of cycles changed significantly: in the light of this, studies that attempt to model cyclical regularity over the long run are clearly misleading.
- Interwar fluctuations were influenced both by real and monetary shocks. Theoretical models that attempt to explain business cycles in terms of monetary theory or real business cycle theory both have a contribution to make. This result is in marked contrast to studies of the pre-1914 gold standard era which show that monetary shocks were unimportant in accounting for economic fluctuations (Capie and Mills, 1992; Catao and Solomou, 1993). Thus contrasting long-run comparisons suggest that the exchange rate regimes of the interwar era introduced far more policy discretion than was observed under the classical gold standard.
- The processes generating cycles and economic growth are difficult to disentangle. The shocks generating business cycles also generated more permanent effects on the macro-economy. These effects are particularly important in the depression of 1920–1.

APPENDIX 1   DATA RELIABILITY AND BUSINESS CYCLE ANALYSIS

In describing the characteristics of interwar business cycles we should note a number of important points concerning the reliability of interwar macroeconomic data. Figure A4.1 plots the discrepancy between the income and expenditure estimates of GDP during 1920–38: the size of the discrepancy was over 7 per cent of GDP in the early 1920s, and fell to about 2 per cent between 1928 and 1938. Although lower than those for the pre-1914 era, these discrepancies are still large enough to affect our understanding of business cycle behaviour.

Economic historians have attempted to deal with this problem by using the compromise estimate (an average of the income, expenditure and output estimates of GDP) to describe the path of the macroeconomy. If we assume the measurement errors to be random and the three estimates of GDP of equal reliability, the compromise estimate may provide a practical and simple aggregate solution to these measurement error problems. However, neither of these assumptions are valid: the interwar aggregate measurement errors are autocorrelated and the three estimates of real GDP differ in their reliability (Solomou and Weale, 1993).

The existence of autocorrelation in the error process means that we cannot easily distinguish the true cyclical process by describing the observed data. The autocorrelation in the measurement error is a product of the data generation processes used in putting together the interwar national accounts. The methods of extrapolation, interpolation and deflation, which are used to generate annual national income estimates also generate an autocorrelated measurement error in the component series. The data that we use in this chapter are the balanced national accounts put together by Solomou and Weale (1993). Instead of taking a simple average, as in the construction of the

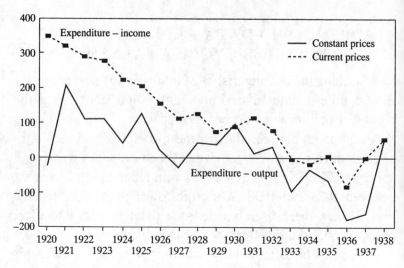

Figure A4.1: Residual errors in GDP (millions of pounds)

compromise estimate, regression methods are used, together with the reliability values of each component series and the autocorrelation structure imposed on the error of each series, to produce a disaggregated system of national accounts that satisfy national accounting constraints. A further important advantage of this method is that an adjustment is made to the components and not just to the aggregate GDP series.

APPENDIX 2   BUSINESS CYCLE THEORY

Two strands of business cycle theory have been extensively discussed in the recent theoretical literature: the monetary and real business cycle perspectives. Let us consider each in turn:

THE MONETARY THEORY OF BUSINESS CYCLES

The idea that unanticipated monetary shocks can generate real fluctuations has seen a revival in the rational expectations literature (Lucas, 1981; Barro, 1981). The basic theoretical premise is that transitory monetary shocks induce rational agents to change their real behaviour with respect to work and leisure and consumption and investment. Since gathering information has a cost, even with rational expectations, individuals do not acquire all information instantaneously; thus, absolute price changes are likely to be mistaken for relative price changes. Hence, inflationary monetary shocks are likely to have expansionary cyclical effects. Let us consider Lucas' model as an example of how random monetary shocks are propagated to generate economic cycles (Lucas, 1981). The model consists of the following structure:

$$Y_t = Y_n + \alpha(P_t - P_t^*) + \varepsilon_t \tag{1}$$
$$Y_n = \delta + \gamma \text{ TREND} \tag{2}$$
$$Y_{ct} = \alpha(P_t - P_t^*) + \varepsilon_t \tag{3}$$

where

Y_t = real national income
Y_n = steady state income level
Y_{ct} = cyclical component of the economy
ε_t = random shock variable, $\varepsilon_t \sim (0,\sigma^2)$
P_t = actual price level
P_t^* = rational expectations prediction of the price level given available information.

Equation (1) implies that the economy has a tendency, once shocked, to return to the steady state path. Cycles are the result of changes in the price level due to unanticipated monetary shocks. Lucas employs the 'island markets' parable to illustrate how this comes about: the general idea behind this concept is that individuals have incomplete information due to the cost of gathering and processing relevant information. Limited information generates a 'signal extraction problem' and producers are likely to misinterpret an absolute price change, due to an unanticipated inflationary monetary shock, as a relative price change which then leads to real effects in the short term. In this model an unanticipated monetary shock is simply inflationary, explicable within a quantity theory framework; however, the information problem means that individuals think that profit rates have risen because prices have risen. A propagation mechanism is thus set off with investment and labour supply rising. As more information is processed individuals will realise that the rise in prices was a general inflationary shock and the current level of investment and labour supply is above the optimum level, leading to downward cyclical adjustments in the future.

This model can produce an explanation for some of the features of business cycles, including irregular cyclical data and a co-movement of macroeconomic variables. However, a number of key features of business cycles are inadequately captured by the framework. The assumption of a unique steady-state equilibrium path is unfounded: there now exists much evidence showing that twentieth-century macroeconomic data has followed a 'random walk',* or at least a number of segmented trend* breaks. The model focuses on supply responses, neglecting demand: if we consider a more symmetric model of supply and demand, a far more damped cycle is observed. This arises because although the belief that a current price or wage is high represents a perceived high profit opportunity and a high real wage for the suppliers of goods and labour, it represents a corresponding bad deal for consumers and employers. Hence, outward shifts in supply are counter-balanced by inward shifts in demand.

REAL BUSINESS CYCLE (RBC) THEORY

In an attempt to deal with these problems the 1980s saw the development of real business cycle theory. Instead of focusing on monetary shocks the real business cycle literature has emphasised the importance of real (technological) shocks. The theory has three main features: first, in recognition of the random walk in output the analyses of growth and cycles are integrated within the same framework. Both processes are driven by technology and technological shocks. Secondly, the theory emphasises the role of impulses in generating cycles, as against endogenous economic processes. Finally, the theory offers an equilibrium analysis of business cycles; the actual path that the economy follows is the equilibrium path. Business cycles are, thus, the result of optimising behaviour by individuals.

In order to illustrate the basic strands of RBC theory consider the effects of a favourable (but random) technological shock. Since technological improvement raises productivity and output the shock allows the representative consumer to increase consumption now. However the individual also values extra consumption in the future; intertemporal decision making should result in an increase in investment as a way of raising future consumption. An increase of investment is also expected from the decision making of the representative firm: since the shock is random, it is impossible for the firm to distinguish *ex ante* whether a shock is permanent or transitory. By its very nature the effects of innovation are uncertain: hence, the shock may also signal high productivity in the future. The only way the firm can hedge against this contingency is to initiate investment in the current period. This stylised outline shows that even a *random* technological shock will have cyclical effects.

The model can be extended to consider the effects of persistent technology shocks. A growth process can be specified as (all variables in logs)

$$Y_t = \alpha + \beta Y_{t-1} + U_t \qquad (4)$$

Y_t = aggregate output
U_t = path of technology

In order to allow for the random walk in output, consider a technology path that follows a random walk,

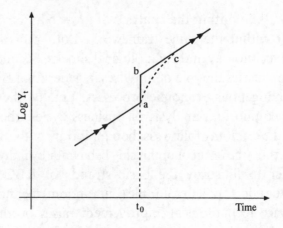

Figure A4.2: The effect of a permanent technology shock

$$U_t = g + U_{t-1} + \varepsilon_t \tag{5}$$

Equation (5) models technology as growing at a rate of g with a random walk in the level of technology. For example, the railways can be seen as a permanent addition to the level of technology and the oil shocks of the 1970s can be seen as having a persistent negative effect on the level of existing technology. Equations (4) and (5) yield a growth process illustrated in figure A4.2. A favourable technology shock at t_0 will displace the level of aggregate output along the path ab. However, in a world of intertemporal decision making, the process of consumption smoothing will mean that it is more likely that the economy will traverse along ac. By explicitly trying to explain the growth-cycle process within the same framework real business cycle theory offers an explanation for the random walk in aggregate output which the monetary theory cannot do. However, it should be emphasised that both theories share similar features in that they are market clearing theories of business cycles; thus, it is possible to integrate both theories within an encompassing framework as Lucas (1988) has shown.

SELECTED FURTHER READING

Backus, D.K. and Kehoe, P.J. (1992), 'International Evidence on the Historical Properties of Business Cycles', *American Economic Review*.

Corner, D.C. (1956), 'British Exports and the British Trade Cycle: 1929', *The Manchester School of Economics and Social Studies*.

Dowie J. (1975), '1919–20 is in Need of Attention', *Economic History Review*.

Fremdling, G. (1985), 'Did the US Transmit the Great Depression to the Rest of the World?', *American Economic Review*.

Hicks, J.R. (1974), 'Real and Monetary Factors in Economic Fluctuations', *Scottish Journal of Political Economy*.

Mills, T. (1991), 'Are Fluctuations in UK Output Transitory or Permanent?', *The Manchester School*.

Solomou, S.N. and Weale, M. (1996), 'UK National Income 1920–1938', *Economic History Review*.

CHAPTER 5

EXCHANGE RATE REGIMES AND ECONOMIC RECOVERY IN THE 1930s

INTRODUCTION

The 1930s witnessed a number of major policy shifts: the government devalued sterling in September 1931 and replaced the high interest rate policy of the 1920s with a 'cheap money' policy between 1932 and 1939; the protection of the manufacturing sector was extended significantly in 1932 breaking away from a long tradition of unilateral free trade; the international payments system was transformed from a fixed exchange rate regime between 1925 and 1931 to a managed exchange rate after devaluation. This chapter focuses on the effects of exchange rate policy on economic performance during the 1930s. However, it should be noted that the occurrence of a number of policy changes at a similar point in time makes it extremely difficult to distinguish individual policy impacts.

In this chapter the experience of the UK is analysed using the comparative approach developed by Choudri and Kochin (1980) and Eichengreen and Sachs (1985). During this period the world economy can usefully be divided into at least two groups of countries: those that devalued and came off gold in the early 1930s, such as the UK, and the 'gold bloc', a group of countries that remained committed to the fixed gold parity they had established in the 1920s. The major countries in this latter group included Belgium, France, Italy, the Netherlands and Switzerland. The cross-sectional differences in the economic performance of these exchange rate policy zones provide interesting insights into the effects of devaluation and the propagation mechanisms by which these came about.

UK ECONOMIC PERFORMANCE DURING THE 1930s

Much of the industrialised world experienced retarded economic growth in the 1930s relative to the 1920s: this was the common experience of Austria, Belgium, Canada, Denmark, France, Italy, Japan, the Netherlands, Switzerland and America, not to mention many of the poorer nations of the world. The UK, on the other hand, continued to grow on a steady path when compared to the 1920s and saw some improvement when comparisons are made with 1913–29 or 1899–1929.

Figure 5.1 plots the interperiod growth changes for a selection of countries. The interperiod growth comparison between 1913–29 and 1929–37 provides a measure of the difference in the rate of economic growth during 1929–37 relative to the underlying growth path observed between 1913–29.[1] Of the fifteen leading economies covered eleven saw a fall in economic growth in the 1930s relative to 1913–29. Only Finland, Germany and the UK performed substantially better; Norway and Australia performed marginally better. In terms of this measure of *change* in economic performance the UK is at the top of a rank-ordering of the major countries in the world economy; the 1930s saw a trend improvement in the UK economy both in terms of comparisons with other countries

---

[1] Given that GDP growth varied significantly across countries, reflecting different national-specific shocks and supply-side (natural growth) potentials, the absolute differences in interperiod growth rates were scaled by dividing with the average long-run growth of each country for the period 1913–29. Such a scaling allows us to focus on relative changes over time and across countries.

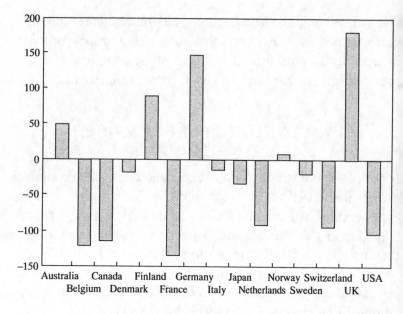

Figure 5.1: Growth performance, 1930s (inter-period per cent changes)

and relative to the poor performance of 1913–29. Similar cross-sectional results also hold when interperiod comparisons are made between 1929–37 and 1924–9: while UK gross domestic product continued to grow on a path of 2 per cent per annum during 1929–37, many other countries saw growth retardation in the 1930s.

Figure 5.2 plots the annual growth rate of the major industrial countries during the trough to peak period of the 1930s business cycle. The UK growth performance is near the median of this distribution, averaging 4 per cent per annum. However, we would expect the strength of cyclical recovery to be related to the severity of depression; countries with severe depressions are expected to see higher growth rates in the recovery phase of the cycle, reflecting high levels of excess capacity resulting from the depression. In the light of the fact that the amplitude of the UK depression during 1929–32 was

114

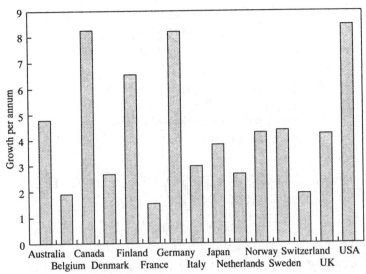

Figure 5.2: Cyclical growth rates (growth per annum, 1932–7)

comparatively mild a median position represents a significant climb in the international growth leagues. Moreover, all the major countries that saw higher cyclical growth than the UK experienced depressions of an exceptionally high amplitude (including Canada, Germany and the USA). UK GDP growth averaged 4 per cent per annum throughout 1932–7; this rate had not been achieved during any other five-year period since 1856 (the earliest period for which we have annual GDP estimates).

Summarising the evidence considered so far: the economic performance of the UK in the 1930s, whether looked at from a short-run business cycle perspective, a medium-term comparison with the 1920s or a longer run comparison with the period 1913–29 shows significant improvement. This does not mean that the experience of the UK was unique. However, what is clear is that for the first time in fifty years UK relative economic performance was moving up the international growth ladder.

Table 5.1. Exchange rates and GDP growth
(per cent growth per annum)

	Gold bloc	Devaluers
1913–29	2.09	2.17
1929–37	0.32	1.68

Source: Maddison (1982).

EXCHANGE RATES AND ECONOMIC PERFORMANCE IN THE 1930s

As noted above the policy regimes of the world economy during the 1930s can be dichotomised into the 'gold bloc' and the devaluing economies. While the average growth rates of these exchange rate blocs were similar during 1913–29 (and 1924–9) they saw marked differences in the 1930s. As can be seen from tables 5.1–5.3 the devaluing countries were far more successful in sustaining long-run economic growth than the gold bloc economies. Eichengreen (1991) provides evidence for a cross-section of countries for which we have data. His classification distinguishes four exchange rate zones, partly to reflect the new economic and trading blocs that developed in the 1930s and the different external constraints to economic growth. He distinguishes the following zones: the gold bloc, the exchange control countries, the sterling bloc and other depreciators. The results, reported in table 5.4, show that during 1929–35 and 1929–36 the sterling bloc* and the other devaluers grew much faster than the gold bloc and the exchange control countries.

In theoretical terms it is useful to distinguish between the cyclical and long-run effects arising from the exchange rate regime. In choosing the period of their analysis Eichengreen and Sachs (1985) work with the benchmark years of 1929 and 1935 which may confuse this distinction. The argument for

116

Table 5.2. GDP growth rates of gold bloc and devaluers, 1913–37 (growth per annum)

	1913–29 (%)	1929–37 (%)
Gold bloc		
Belgium	1.42	0.25
France	1.44	−0.51
Italy	1.66	1.42
Netherlands	3.19	0.26
Switzerland	2.72	0.16
Average	2.09	0.32
Devaluers		
Australia	1.30	1.93
Austria	0.31	−1.82
Canada	2.42	−0.37
Denmark	2.66	2.18
Finland	2.81	4.11
Germany[a]	1.20	3.00
Japan	3.64	2.37
Norway	2.88	3.08
Sweden	2.80	2.20
UK	0.70	1.96
USA	3.10	−0.16
Average	2.17	1.68

Note: [a] Germany imposed exchange controls.
Source: Maddison (1982).

choosing 1935 as the endpoint is that rearmament was very important after that date and most countries had left the gold bloc by 1935 (the major exception being France). However, economies were continuously subjected to shocks; in this respect the period 1929–35, and particularly the period 1929–33,

Table 5.3. GDP growth rates of gold bloc and devaluers,
1932–7 (per cent growth per annum)

	Growth rate 1932–7 (%)	Amplitude of depression 1929–32
Gold bloc		
Belgium	1.86	−2.45
France	1.51	−3.87
Italy[a]	2.94	−1.28
Netherlands[b]	2.65	−1.96
Switzerland	1.91	−2.76
Devaluers		
Australia	4.75	−1.52
Canada	8.21	−9.65
Denmark	2.64	1.41
Finland	6.50	−1.44
Germany	8.16	−5.72
Japan	3.77	−1.08
Norway[a]	4.27	1.84
Sweden	4.34	−1.37
UK	4.18	−1.74
USA[b]	8.42	−10.97

Notes:
[a] The specific cycle dates are 1931–7.
[b] The specific cycle dates are 1933–7.
Source: Maddison (1982).

faced as many major shocks as the years after 1935. Moreover, an interesting question to consider is whether the exchange rate regime had some *persistent* effects on macroeconomic performance: even though most countries had left the gold bloc by 1935 the economic legacies of staying on gold during 1931–5 (1936 for France) clearly stretched beyond 1935.

Such growth comparisons between the gold bloc and the

Table 5.4. Percentage change in industrial production, 1929–36

	1929–32	1929–33	1929–34	1929–35	1929–36
Gold bloc	−28.2	−22.6	−21.8	−20.6	−13.9
Exchange control	−35.7	−31.7	−21.2	−10.3	−2.3
Sterling bloc	−8.8	−2.5	8.9	18.1	27.8
Other depreciators	−17.5	−1.6	3.3	14.1	27.1

Source: Eichengreen (1991).

devaluing countries suggest that the exchange rate regime was a major influence on economic performance. However, the differential in growth rates between the two policy zones cannot be solely attributed to exchange rate policies. In the remainder of this section I shall address the specific question: *to what extent did the exchange rate regime influence cyclical recovery in the 1930s?* The focus on cyclical recovery reflects the research focus of the existing literature. In order to control for the effect of the depression on cyclical economic performance the following cross-sectional regression model was estimated

$$g_{ti} = a + b \text{ Regime} + c \text{ Amplitude} + \varepsilon_t$$
$$g_{ti} = \text{growth change for 1932–7 by country}$$

Regime = 1,0 dummy variable to distinguish the gold bloc from the devaluing economies
Amplitude = Amplitude of 1929–32 depression by country

The model allows us to distinguish the mean growth performance of the gold bloc economies, controlling for the effect of the level of excess capacity created by the world depression. The results of this model (reported in table 5.5) suggest that the exchange rate regime had a large (and statistically significant) effect on the strength of cyclical recovery. Controlling for the

Table 5.5. Policy regime effects on cyclical recovery of GDP, 1932–7: regression estimates (t values in parentheses)

Parameter	Estimated co-efficient	t ratio
$\hat{a}$	1.17	(2.36)
$\hat{b}$	3.12	(5.57)
$\hat{c}$	−0.41	−(5.30)
$\bar{R}^2$=0.82 F=32.0		

Notes: Model estimated:
$g_{ti}=a+b$ Regime+c Amplitude+ε_t
g_{ti}=national growth rates for 1932–7 (i=1,15).
Regime=1,0 dummy variable to separate the gold bloc from the devaluing economies.
Amplitude=amplitude of 1929–32 depression.
Source: Maddison (1982). For a listing of the countries see table 5.2 above.

amplitude of the depression, the average rate of economic growth of the non-gold bloc countries was 3 percentage points greater than the performance of the gold bloc. Such results are unable to tell us very much about the specific transmission mechanisms by which devaluation provided a stimulus to cyclical recovery. The next section considers three possible linkages:

• Export performance
• Monetary policy
• Labour market effects

EXPORT PERFORMANCE

The most direct effect of devaluation is expected to be on trade flows. By stimulating export growth the devaluing economies may have benefited from an increase in this component of expenditure. Eichengreen and Sachs (1985) find a significant effect in their ten-country study: countries which devalued heir currencies in the early 1930s succeeded in promoting ecovery of export volumes compared to countries that remained committed to the gold standard. As noted above, the Eichengreen and Sachs study relates to the period 1929–35; since the focus of this chapter is on the cyclical recovery effects of devaluation he effect of the exchange rate regime on export performance was analysed over the complete cyclical recovery phase (1932–7).

In contrast to the results of Eichengreen and Sachs during he period 1932–7 the exchange rate regime did not have a ignificant effect on the cyclical recovery path of exports: the gold bloc and the devaluing countries had a comparable poor export performance (see the results reported in table 5.6). The evidence suggests that export growth during the 1930s was determined by factors such as protectionism, the formation of discriminatory trading blocs and the collapse of overseas nvestment, none of which bear any direct relation to particular exchange rate regimes. Moreover, although a nominal devalu- ation gave an initial competitive advantage to the early devaluers, by 1937 this was eliminated as a result of higher nflation rates in the early devaluing countries and by the levaluation of the gold bloc (Eichengreen and Sachs, 1985). Another relevant feature is that trade in the 1930s was ncreasingly being conducted in trading blocs with similar exchange rate strategies; hence, effective exchange rate changes vere significantly more damped than bilateral and interbloc ates (Redmond, 1988). The effect of devaluation on exports is imited to an *impact effect* in the early recovery phase of 932–5: the early export recovery of the devaluing countries vas better than the gold bloc economies.

Focusing on the experience of the UK, the increase in exports during the recovery phase of 1932–7 was not large enough to compensate for the large fall in expenditures during he depression period of 1929–32: hence the volume of exports n 1937 was only 80 per cent of the level of 1929. The strength of

Table 5.6. Policy regime effects on cyclical recovery of
exports, 1932–7: regression estimates (t-values in parentheses)

Parameter	Estimated co-efficient	t ratio
$\hat{a}$	5.34	(2.57)
$\hat{b}$	2.12	(0.85)
$\hat{c}$	−10.10	−(2.2)
$\bar{R}^2=0.36$ F=3.7		

Notes: Model estimated:
$g_{ti}=a+b$ Regime$+c$ Germany$+\varepsilon_t$
g_{ti}=Export growth rates for 1932–7 (i=1,15).
Regime=1,0 dummy variable to separate the gold bloc from the devaluing
economies.
Germany=Dummy variable to capture the policy of autarky in Germany.
Source: Maddison (1982). For a listing of the countries see table 5.2 above.

the cyclical recovery in the UK cannot possibly be explained by
a rapid growth of exports in the 1930s. During the early
recovery phase of 1932–5, however, a revival of exports gave a
kick to the economy out of depression.

In order to determine the magnitude of this impact effect of
devaluation via the trade mechanism Broadberry (1986) uses
the elasticities approach to the balance of payments to analyse
the impact of devaluation on the balance of trade. The effective
exchange rate measures (reported in the appendix to this
chapter) show that the magnitude of devaluation peaked in
1931–2 at 13 per cent. Using the same assumptions about the
pricing responses of importers and exporters (often referred to
as 'pass-through' assumptions) as were made by Moggridge
(1972) in his analysis of the effects of overvaluation in the
1920s, Broadberry estimates an £80 million improvement in
the balance of trade. With a multiplier of 1.75 the impact effect
on GDP is estimated at £140 million (3 per cent of GDP).
There is clearly a significant devaluation effect on trade flows

and GDP that helps to explain the turning point from depression to recovery in 1932.

By the mid 1930s the large competitiveness gain of 1931–2 was being eliminated with an appreciation of the real effective exchange rate. As is well recognised in the conventional international economics literature a nominal one-off devaluation has an *impact effect* on trade which is gradually eliminated by the inflationary effects of the devaluation. In the 1930s this process was speeded up by the competitive devaluations of other countries and other inflationary policies in the domestic economy (such as expansionary monetary policy).

The focus on export performance provides an incomplete picture of the full effects of devaluation. Recent developments in trade theory have emphasised the existence of hysteresis* effects by which a large transitory change in competitiveness can have favourable persistent effects on the economy. By shifting the nature of competition in favour of domestic producers, foreign producers may lose market shares on a permanent basis either because short-run increasing returns to production provide a basis for reinforcing the short-term gains to domestic producers or because domestic producers respond to the resulting appreciation of the real exchange rate by varying their mark-ups. A higher market share for domestic producers allows them to increase the scale of production, lowering unit costs of production. This places the home producers in a stronger position to respond to competitiveness changes for some time in the future. The behaviour of import shares in the 1930s suggests that such effects were present: following the large competitiveness gains of 1931–2 import shares fell on a permanent basis despite the appreciation of the real exchange rate (see figure 5.3). In this light the devaluation and tariff policies can be seen as complementary policies in the short run, giving domestic producers a large competitiveness gain that had more permanent effects during the 1930s.

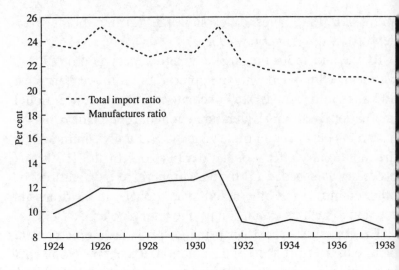

Figure 5.3: Import ratios, 1924–38 (total imports and manufacturing imports)

MONETARY POLICY

Prior to the devaluations of 1931 monetary policy in many European countries had been assigned to sustaining the fixed exchange rate regime. In order to defend the gold standard regime, real interest rates for the four major industrial countries (USA, UK, France and Germany) rose from a mean of 3.7 per cent during 1924–9 to 10.5 per cent during 1930–2. Once devaluation occurred monetary policy was potentially freed as a viable policy instrument: the result was a major difference in the monetary policy stance of the countries leaving the gold standard relative to the gold bloc.[2] By 1933 a large differential had emerged in the monetary policy indicators of these two exchange rate zones: while the gold bloc witnessed monetary

[2] The fiscal impact of devaluation should also be noted. Expenditure switching to the home economy would raise domestic incomes which could improve the budget deficit. If a government follows a balanced budget rule it could, then, cut taxes or raise expenditure giving a further expansionary effect.

ontraction the devaluers saw expansion of money supply and alling interest rates. Eichengreen (1992) notes, however, the hesitation amongst the devaluers in following expansionary monetary policies. The difference between the two exchange ate zones only became significant after a two-year lag, reflecting the slow response of policymakers, given the underlying fear that devaluation would lead to inflation. Once it became clear that devaluation did not lead to high inflation in the 1930s expansionary monetary policies followed.

Focusing on the UK experience, there is evidence that monetary policy was expansionist with a much shorter lag than was observed for many other countries. The depreciation of the exchange rate allowed the government to pursue a more expansionist ('Cheap Money') monetary policy after 1932. Although cheap money was initially a policy for reducing the size of the national debt (the government forced interest rates down as a means of converting the war loan stock of 1917 at 5 per cent to a conversion stock at 3.5 per cent), it has also been seen as a permissive policy for economic revival (Richardson, 1967). The major problem faced by analysts of the effects of the cheap money policy is in documenting a convincing transmission mechanism from monetary policy to the real economy. Although the bank rate remained at the low level of 2 per cent throughout 1932-9, there was no increase in bank advances to industry until 1935. Nevertheless, cheap money could have stimulated recovery directly by stimulating consumption expenditure and by its influence on the housing sector (Broadberry, 1986).

Two mechanisms have been emphasised with respect to the latter link. First, falling interest rates gave rise to a reallocation of savings, with housing investment benefiting because of the more stable returns on housing in the interwar period. Secondly, prior to 1932 the rate of return on building society shares was comparable to that on consols. However, the war loan conversion opened up a gap in favour of building societies; thus building societies had an excess of funds which resulted in favourable mortgage terms. The empirical evidence rejects the importance of this transmission mechanism: building society deposits in fact grew faster in the 1920s than in the 1930s due to an increase in the proportion of savings going to building societies and a peak in repayments. Hence, the availability of funds in the 1930s was mainly due to the favourable conditions of the 1920s, not the monetary policy shift of 1932 (Humphries, 1987).

Broadberry (1987) finds that cheap money accounted for about half of the rise in housing investment in the early phase of the recovery. Nevertheless, even if such a link between policy and the housing boom could be established, the contribution of housing to the revival of the 1930s needs to be kept in perspective. The relative contribution of building and construction to GDP growth declined in the 1930s relative to the 1920s: during 1924-9 this sector accounted for 12.5 per cent of the overall GDP growth rate, a contribution which fell to 8.7 per cent during 1932-3 (Kitson and Solomou, 1990). In contrast, manufacturing industries accounted for 35.6 per cent and 46.6 per cent of the GDP growth rate in the two periods respectively. This is not to deny the critical role of housing in the early stages of recovery. Although housing accounted for only 3 per cent of GDP it accounted for 17 per cent of the *change* in GDP between 1932 and 1934; in terms of employment building accounted for 7.5 per cent of total employment but 20 per cent of the *increase* in employment between 1932 and 1935 (Worswick, 1984).

The comparative evidence suggests that the monetary policy stance of countries leaving the gold standard gave a significant stimulus to their economies. Although the direct effects of expansionary monetary policy on the UK recovery seem weak, the indirect channels of influence are more important. The expansionary monetary policy stance of the UK during the

1930s allowed prices to recover more quickly than the gold bloc economies, improving profitability. Lower interest rates resulted in a rapid revival of the stock market, improving the availability of funds to industry. The fall in building society rates (from 6 per cent in 1931 to 3.5 per cent in 1935) also had a significant effect in lowering the cost of repayment which stimulated the demand for housing and other consumer durables. Bowden (1988) finds that cheap money and the rise in real incomes both contributed to the rapid growth of consumer durable demand in the 1930s.

LABOUR MARKET EFFECTS

Eichengreen and Sachs (1985) find that countries devaluing their currencies experienced lower real-wage growth than the gold bloc economies. If nominal wages are rigid, the inflationary effects of devaluation (both via the trade channel and macro-economic policy effects) would result in lower real-wage growth. Deflating nominal wages by wholesale prices gives some support to this idea: the devaluing countries saw a fall of real wages during 1932–5 while the gold bloc countries saw an increase. However, it is well recognised that deflating by wholesale prices may not be an appropriate way of measuring the cost of labour to the firm. Eichengreen and Hatton (1988) have constructed real-wage indices for a number of countries based on deflating by the relevant product prices, to estimate product real wages for manufacturing. These are plotted in figure 5.4. The paths of economic recovery and real-wage *growth* do not always agree with the wage moderation thesis. Real-wage growth moderated after 1932 in the UK, suggesting a lagged relationship with economic recovery in 1932. However, in the case of Germany and America the timing of recovery is not correlated with wage moderation, even with a lag.

127

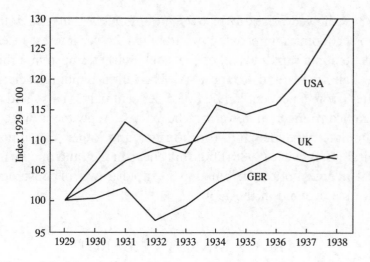

Figure 5.4: Manufacturing real wages (product real wage: 1929 = 100)

CONCLUSIONS

- Exchange rate policies in the 1930s were partly the outcome of exchange rate policies in the 1920s: the early devaluers in the 1930s were the overvalued currencies of the 1920s. The paradox is that countries that controlled inflation in the 1920s (at a high socioeconomic cost) gained the (unintended) policy option of leaving the gold standard in the adverse circumstances of the world depression during the 1930s. The credibility of policy-makers in controlling inflation during the 1920s gave them (unintended) policy flexibility in the 1930s.

- The policy of devaluation, and, thus, the new policy regime that was possible gave the devaluers a major cyclical growth stimulus. Initially this was observed in the form of a better export performance, relative to the gold bloc. However, the more persistent advantage arose from freeing monetary policy from sustaining the gold standard exchange rates.

128

- The long-run effects of exchange rate policies in the 1930s have received less attention in the literature. However, the picture we have is suggestive: countries that left the gold standard early had a better medium-term growth record during the 1930s than the gold bloc and countries devaluing late (such as the USA). Persisting with the gold standard resulted in depressions of a high amplitude, partly because of the deflationist policies needed to sustain the exchange rate regime, the rise in real indebtedness arising from price deflation and the collapse of financial institutions (Bernanke and James, 1991).

APPENDIX   THE MAGNITUDE OF REAL DEVALUATION

The initial devaluation of sterling against the major currencies was significant: the depreciation against the dollar, which had remained on gold until 1933, was 25 per cent (from $4.86 to $3.75) in the first week of trading, continuing to reach a low of $3.19 in December 1932. Table 5A.1 presents a number of different exchange rate measures for the period 1924–38. This shows how misleading it is to focus only on bilateral exchange rates in a world trading system that was retreating into a number of exchange rate blocs, as was the case in the 1930s. While the competitive advantage of the pound against the dollar was lost with the US devaluation of 1933 a significant advantage remained with respect to other countries. The competitive advantage of the UK peaked in 1932; during 1933–7 a significant nominal and real appreciation is observed.

129

Table 5A.1. Sterling exchange rate measures

	(1) Sterling-dollar	(2) Sterling effective exchange rate	(3) Sterling average exchange rate	(4) Sterling manufacturing exchange
1924	91.0		84.6	83.0
1925	99.5		93.5	91.4
1926	100.1		102.3	101.6
1927	100.1		100.0	100.1
1928	100.2		100.0	100.0
1929	100.0	100.0	100.0	100.0
1930	100.1		99.6	100.1
1931	93.4	100.1	93.7	94.8
1932	72.2	86.7	75.2	75.7
1933	87.3	91.3	77.0	83.8
1934	103.8	95.9	75.4	86.0
1935	100.1	95.4	74.5	85.5
1936	102.4	97.5	77.7	88.5
1937	101.8	100.8	84.7	94.3
1938	100.7	105.1	86.9	100.3

Notes: 1929 = 100 except for the sterling effective exchange rate where 1929–30=100.

Sources: column (1) Svennilson (1954), pp. 318–19; column (2) Redmond (1980), appendix; column (3) Dimsdale (1981), tables 3 and 9; column (4) Svennilson (1954), pp. 318–19, LCES (various editions) and Board of Trade (1929 and 1939). Countries covered are USA, France, Germany, Belgium, Netherlands, Canada, Australia and India. Weights are average share of UK manufacturing trade for 1928 and 1935. For a fuller description see Kitson and Solomou (1990), chapter 4.

SELECTED FURTHER READING

Broadberry, S.N. (1986), *The British Economy Between the Wars: A Macroeconomic Survey* (chapters 12, 14 and 15).

Dimsdale, N. (1981), 'British Monetary Policy and the Exchange rate 1920–38', in Eltis, W.A. and Sinclair, P.J.N. (eds.), *The Money Supply and the Exchange Rate*.

Eichengreen, B. and Sachs, J. (1985), 'Exchange Rates and Economic Recovery in the 1930s', *Journal of Economic History*.

Kitson, M. and Solomou, S.N. (1990), *Protectionism and Economic Revival* (chapter 6).

Redmond, J. (1980), 'An Indicator of the Effective Exchange Rate of the Pound in the 1930s', *Economic History Review*.

Thomas, M. 'The Macro-economics of the Interwar Years', in Floud, R. and McCloskey, D.N., *The Economic History of Britain Since 1700*, vol. II.

CHAPTER 6

PROTECTION AND ECONOMIC REVIVAL IN THE 1930s

In February 1932 the UK imposed a General Tariff of 10 per cent *ad valorem** on imports from foreign countries: this amounted to a clear protectionist device designed to shield the domestic industrial sector from foreign competition. To appreciate fully the nature of the change in the UK's trade policy we need to place it in the wider context of protectionism in the world economy. The UK was the only major industrial country to pursue a *unilateral* free trade policy in the period 1870–1913. Even by 1925 the limited extent of protection in the UK (see table 6.1) meant that the average tariff level on manufactured goods was only 5 per cent *ad valorem*: the McKenna Duties* (1915) and the Safeguarding of Industries Act (1921) had already protected some of the new industries such as motor cars, chemicals and scientific instruments. In contrast, the average tariff for Continental Europe was 25 per cent (Liepmann, 1938) and for the United States 37 per cent (Bairoch, 1986; Eichengreen, 1989).

The early 1930s saw a sharp rise in tariff levels and quotas throughout the world economy (see figure 6.1), initially induced by falling food and raw material prices in 1928–9 which forced many European countries to raise the level of agricultural protection in order to alleviate distress in the sector. Under the Smoot-Hawley tariff in 1930 the level of American tariff

Table 6.1. Average tariff levels of European countries, 1913,
1927 and 1932 (per cent)

	1913	1927	1931
Germany	16.7	20.4	40.7
France	23.6	23.0	38.0
Italy	24.8	27.8	48.3
Belgium	14.2	11.0	17.4
Switzerland	10.5	16.8	26.4
Sweden	27.6	20.0	26.8
Finland	35.0	31.8	48.2
Spain	37.0	49.0	68.5
Austria	22.8	17.5	36.0
Czechoslovakia	22.8	31.3	50.0
Hungary	22.8	30.0	45.0
Bulgaria	22.8	67.5	96.5
Poland	–	53.5	67.5
Romania	30.3	42.3	63.0
Yugoslavia	–	32.0	46.0
UK	–	4.0	17.0

Sources: Liepman (1938, p. 415) and Kitson and Solomou (1990, pp. 65–6).

protection also reached unprecedented heights, especially for manufactured goods, with an average duty of 45 to 50 per cent (Eichengreen, 1989). Before the end of 1931, partly as a reprisal to the US measures, twenty-five countries had raised their duties on American products. Such trends suggest that to analyse the effects of the General Tariff the relevant question that needs to be addressed is whether the UK pursued an appropriate *second best** trade policy in the 1930s: the world trading system was already highly distorted. A policy of continuing with *unilateral* free trade, which assumes no existing distortions, was simply not viable in the circumstances of the 1930s.

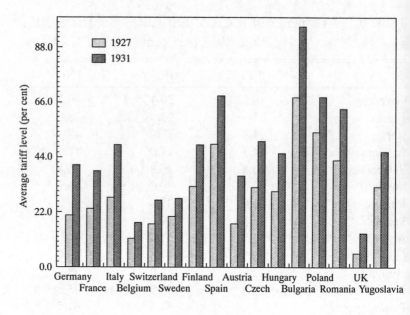

Figure 6.1: Average tariff levels (percentage rates for 1927 and 1931)

Given the large number of policy changes in the early 1930s it is difficult to isolate the effects of individual policies: sterling was devalued in 1931 facilitating an expansionary monetary policy after 1932, the same year as the introduction of the General Tariff. The simultaneity of policy changes means that we have to tread carefully in this analysis. In chapter 5 we showed that devaluation policy helps to explain the cross-country cyclical recovery paths in the 1930s. This chapter considers the role of tariffs in contributing to the improved performance of the UK economy during the 1930s.

THEORETICAL ANALYSIS: MICROFOUNDATIONS

The traditional argument for free trade is generally developed in terms of free trade allowing countries to specialise in the production of those goods in which they have comparative advantage. By enlarging consumption possibilities free trade increases the welfare of individual countries and the world economic system. The imposition of tariffs disturbs the optimal allocation of resources, creates a 'dead-weight loss'* on efficiency in the protectionist country and disrupts the equilibrium of the world trading system by creating distortions in the price mechanism. This classical argument for free trade is based on three important assumptions:

- we are dealing with a small open economy that cannot affect world relative prices
- the economy is at full employment without any cyclical adjustment problems
- production operates at constant or diminishing returns to scale and there are no other distortions in the economic system

If any of these assumptions are not satisfied it is possible to make the following arguments in favour of protectionist policies:

(i) The optimum tariff
A country which is large enough (such that it is not a price taker) to affect world prices may find it advantageous to impose a general tariff. When a tariff is imposed there are two opposing forces at work: first, there is a terms of trade effect which is beneficial to the country imposing the tariff; a tariff lowers the demand for foreign goods, resulting in a fall in the price of imports, pushing the terms of trade in favour of the large country imposing the tariff. Secondly, there is a fall in the volume of imports which is harmful, in the sense that a tariff distorts relative prices and consumption behaviour. An optimum tariff is that tariff rate which implies that the benefit due to the former effect outweighs the adverse distortionary effects on consumption.

(ii) Adjustment costs

With its assumption of full employment and instantaneous adjustment to economic shocks, the free trade doctrine can be misleading as a policy guide. Economies are faced with shocks that impose the need for permanent or transitory adjustment. Such shocks may generate cyclical or structural unemployment with large social and economic costs. Moreover, it is now widely recognised that even temporary shocks may have persistent (hysteresis) effects on output and unemployment. If policy-makers are concerned with minimising these socio-economic costs there may be a role for protection as a 'second best' policy. For example, protection may help to minimise the destruction of human and physical capital* by giving industries the necessary time to adjust to new conditions of comparative advantage or to the state of the international business cycle. It may be argued, however, that if this is the policy objective of a government, protection is clearly not the ideal policy response since it is not targeted at the specific problem. For example, if policy-makers wish to slow down the rate of job losses in the short run then an employment subsidy would be a better policy instrument, because it is targeted at the specific problem. Such an argument, however, assumes a high degree of certainty in policy-making which implies that governments can choose the optimal policy instrument and vary it according to needs. Under conditions of uncertainty one may wish to use a more blunt policy instrument by combining a subsidy with some form of protection policy for unanticipated events.

(iii) Increasing returns

The assumptions of imperfect competition and increasing returns to scale* have only recently been successfully integrated into international trade theory. The main necessity is to explain the extensive and growing intra-industry trade* between industrialised countries in the twentieth century: the explanation for intra-industry trade flows is found in the existence of differentiated goods produced under increasing returns. A diversity of taste amongst consumers provides an incentive for product differentiation and the presence of economies of scale leads to each country specialising in a limited number of products. The impact of tariffs in a situation of increasing returns and imperfect competition is contingent on the market structure. The presence of increasing returns implies that price is above marginal cost, giving rise to the possibility of welfare-improving state interventions. Protection may offer a 'second best' instrument for raising welfare. To illustrate this consider the market structure of monopolistic competition. Monopolistic competition* takes place in a setting of a large number of firms producing differentiated products. In equilibrium pure profits are zero. The imposition of tariffs under this market structure increases the profits of domestic firms and lowers the profits of foreign firms. Foreign firms may attempt to avoid the impact of the tariff by setting up production in the domestic economy. Such 'tariff jumping'* increases domestic welfare by increasing product variety and investment in the country imposing the tariff.

These microfoundations for the analysis of trade policy suggest that the free trade paradigm requires very restrictive assumptions to hold if it is to be of use for policy analysis. This chapter considers the hypothesis that the conditions of the interwar did not provide a basis that would have made free trade a sensible or sustainable unilateral national policy for the UK.

MACROECONOMICS OF TARIFFS

One of the first important contributions in this area is Mundell's (1961) seminal paper. Mundell's model suggests that the imposition of a general tariff, in the absence of extensive retaliation, will generate favourable output and employment effects under a system of fixed exchange rates but is ineffective under flexible exchange rates. Consider figure 6.2, which illustrates a fix-price IS-LM model of an open economy. Tariffs initially improve the trade balance shifting the IS curve to the right. Moreover, the improvement in the balance of payments with fixed exchange rates will lead to an expansion of the money supply. The final equilibrium will be a point such as C, with a higher income level. By assuming a fixed exchange rate regime and fixed prices this model depicts point C as a point of macroeconomic equilibrium. However, although a fixed *nominal* exchange rate may be sustained by government intervention, the real exchange rate can appreciate through the inflationary effect of tariffs. This feature of exchange rate 'crowding out' is illustrated explicitly by considering the case of flexible nominal exchange rates (see figure 6.3). The tariff improves the trade balance but at the same time the exchange rate appreciates in response to the effects of the tariff, resulting in an adverse effect on national income and the trade balance. The final equilibrium will be along path AB, depending upon the extent of exchange rate crowding out.

Although the Mundell model has been used to analyse the effects of trade policy in the 1930s (Broadberry, 1986) many of its assumptions are too restrictive to make it operational for analysing the effect of UK tariffs on the cyclical recovery of 1932–7. The most restrictive assumption is that of full employment. In 1932 when the General Tariff was imposed, the UK economy was in the trough of a major world depression. Although the amplitude of the UK depression was mild relative to other countries, excess capacity was clearly present. In these circumstances expansionary income effects would need to be compared to the contractionary price effects. Secondly, the model neglects the specification of the investment relationship: investment is assumed to be exogenous, and

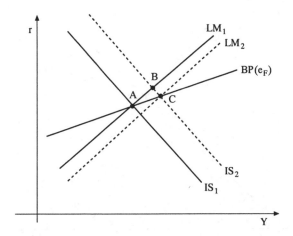

Figure 6.2: Open economy IS-LM model: fixed exchange rates
Notes: A = initial equilibrium; B = A tariff stimulates domestic activity via an improvement in the trade balance. The improvement in the trade balance will result in monetary inflows that will increase domestic money supply, shifting the LM curve to the right; C = Post-tariff equilibrium; e_F = Fixed nominal exchange rate

hence any possible impact flowing from tariffs to investment is ignored. Finally, the model assumes constant returns to scale: the presence of increasing returns means that a one-off competitiveness gain for domestic producers could lead to some *persistent* benefits for the home economy.

In order to develop an operational macroeconomic framework for analysing the impact of the General Tariff we need to make a number of important adaptations to the conventional static macroeconomic models. The following are some aspects we need to consider:

INCREASED COMPETITIVENESS

A tariff changes relative prices, making domestic products more competitive relative to foreign products in the home market. This gives rise to a process of import substitution in domestic production and consumption. The flexibility of the

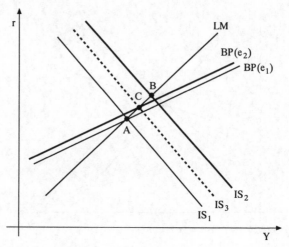

Figure 6.3: Open economy IS-LM model: flexible exchange rates
Notes: A = *initial equilibrium;* B = *A tariff stimulates domestic activity via an*
improvement in the trade balance. This induces an appreciation of the nominal
exchange rate (resulting in an adverse effect on the trade balance); C = *Post-tariff*
equilibrium. The actual position will depend on the extent of crowding out;
e = *Nominal exchange rate which is assumed to vary with the trade balance*

exchange rate during the period 1932–7 was constrained by the
market intervention of the Exchange Equalisation Account*
(EEA) of the Treasury. The system was a *managed* exchange
rate regime: from 1932 the treasury sought to keep the
exchange rate from rising through the exchange rate purchases
of the EEA (Howsen, 1975). The inflationary effects of the
tariff are evaluated below.

INCOME EFFECTS

In circumstances of excess capacity and unemployment a tariff
will result in an increase of domestic incomes which extends
beyond the protected manufacturing sector via the impact of
the intersectoral multiplier. Some of the increase in domestic
incomes will also be leaked abroad in terms of increased
demand for imports. If such income effects are large enough

140

the trade balance need not improve with the imposition of tariffs, invalidating the results of the simple Mundell model, which is based on the assumption of full employment.

INCREASING RETURNS AND HYSTERESIS EFFECTS

The more favourable conditions for manufacturing and the wider domestic market allows some branches of the economy to expand along a path of short-run increasing returns and falling average costs. The relevance of increasing returns will mean that even if the competitiveness gain from the imposition of a general tariff is partly eliminated via an appreciation of the real exchange rate, the short-term gains in competitiveness during the impact period of 1932–3 may have generated favourable persistent effects on the economy. With increasing returns, history matters in determining the path of an economy: once the domestic producers have regained some of the domestic market it may be very difficult for the foreign producers to reenter the market to the same extent as in the past because the long-run average costs of domestic producers have fallen as a result of the policy change. Hence, instead of emphasising the conflict of tariff and devaluation policies (as in the Mundell model), we need to note the complementarity of the two policies in the impact period of 1931–3.

INSTITUTIONAL AND PSYCHOLOGICAL EFFECTS

Under conditions of uncertainty, a major policy shift aimed at guaranteeing a higher level of domestic demand for home producers may increase investment by far more than can be explained by relative price and output shifts. In order to understand this phenomenon tariffs may be viewed as an institution aimed at reducing uncertainty for producers which may account for some non-linearities in the investment accelerator*: investment may be driven more by such expectational (belief) changes than by income changes as predicted by

141

the accelerator theories of investment behaviour. The General Tariff Act of 1932 recognised the importance of such *permanent* guarantees to domestic producers by instituting the Import Duties Advisory Committee with delegated powers to monitor changes in competitiveness and raise tariff levels in the 'national interest'. As a result of this administrative structure, by 1933 the average tariff level had risen from 10 per cent to 18 per cent (Kitson and Solomou, 1990).

EMPIRICAL ANALYSIS AND QUESTIONS

The empirical focus of this chapter will consider the following questions:

- Did tariffs lead to an inflationary effect on the UK economy, relative to other economies, appreciating the real exchange rate and crowding-out the expansionary effects of the General Tariff?
- Did tariffs lead to a process of demand substitution away from imports towards domestic investment and consumer goods?
- Did tariffs generate a process of import substitution in domestic production?
- Did tariffs stimulate the scale-intensive industries?

TARIFFS AND PRICING

The pricing response of domestic and foreign producers to changes in tariff rates is critical to determining the magnitude of change in competitiveness: if domestic producers simply use the protection afforded by tariffs to raise prices and foreign producers respond to the loss of competitiveness by cutting prices, competitiveness may, in fact, be little changed. Such information on the 'pass-through' properties of the tariff

Table 6.2. Imports liable to duty (millions of pounds)

	As declared a	As declared plus duty b	At average values of goods produced domestically c	a/c(%)	b/c(%)
Sample A					
1930	87.2	87.2	91.8	95.0	95.0
1933	31.4	37.1	41.0	76.6	90.5
1934	34.4	40.7	44.2	77.7	92.1
Sample B					
1930	39.6	39.6	49.0	80.8	80.8
1933	19.0	22.5	25.2	75.4	89.0
1934	21.4	25.3	28.6	74.8	88.4

Source: Leak (1937, p. 583).

requires a disaggregated analysis of the pricing behaviour of domestic and foreign firms. This issue has been neglected by economic historians, but was partially addressed in a contemporary Board of Trade analysis of the General Tariff by Leak (1937). Leak considered the impact of the tariff on import prices relative to domestic prices for manufactured goods. A summary of Leak's results is presented in table 6.2. Imports were split up into two categories: the first category, sample A, relates to classes of commodities of which domestic production exceeded £1 million in 1934. Two major features stand out: first, import prices were lower than those for similar domestic products. Secondly, there was a fall of approximately 19 percentage points in the relative price of imports from 1930 to 1933; this corresponds closely to the average duty imposed in 1933. This indicates that the domestic price of imports (average value plus duty) relative to the average value of domestically

143

produced goods was not substantially altered by the tariff (see final column of table 6.2). This would imply that for sample A goods domestic manufacturers took advantage of the tariff to increase prices or that importers decreased their prices by a similar amount, or a combination of both processes.

Sample B was chosen on different criteria, being those goods for which imports in 1930 accounted for at least a third of the domestic market. In 1930 the relation of average values of imports to average values of domestic products was consistently lower for sample B than for sample A.[1] The impact of the tariff was to make the internal price of sample B imports (inclusive of the tariff) some 10 per cent below the price of similar home produced goods compared with 20 per cent below in 1930. Thus in 1933–4, these imports were approximately 10 per cent less competitive in the domestic market compared with 1930. Leak suggested that this relationship prevailed because domestic manufacturers were able to reduce prices due to expanding production.

Leak's evidence on pricing behaviour shows that the inflationary effects of tariffs were not always strong in the depressed conditions of the early 1930s. This result has some intuitive appeal. In a depression period, with a high level of excess capacity, the inflationary effect of tariffs will be expected to be small (Foreman-Peck, 1979). Moreover, under conditions of oligopolistic competition tariffs will lead to falling mark-ups for imported goods, increasing the degree of competition for domestic producers; the existence of economies of scale may encourage domestic producers to keep their new competitive edge against imported goods by *not* raising prices. Finally, the protectionist response of the early 1930s is general to the world economy; what will matter in determining changes in interna-

---

[1] Leak suggests that this may be because a price advantage was required to enter the UK market. However, this may also reflect the pricing strategies of foreign firms in order to take a rising share of the UK market.

144

ional competitiveness is the *relative* impact of tariffs on prices. The average tariff *changes* of France, Germany and America were comparable to those of the UK during 1927–31 (see table 5.1). Thus, although there is clear evidence that the real effective exchange rate appreciated between 1932 and 1937 Broadberry, 1986; Redmond, 1980) this cannot simply be attributed to the effects of the tariff. Moreover, as noted above, he policies of devaluation and tariffs complemented each other in the impact period by giving domestic producers a higher share of the domestic market.

PROTECTION AND MANUFACTURING IMPORTS

Despite a significant growth of national income between 1929–37 imports of manufactures fell by 17.6 per cent, a sharp contrast to the rise of 65.7 per cent between 1920 and 1929. The result was a very large fall in the share of imports of manufactures relative to net manufacturing output (Maizels, 1963; Kitson and Solomou, 1990). The downward shift of imports was also observed for aggregate imports as a proportion of GDP (Matthews *et al.*, 1982; Beenstock and Warburton, 1983). In the face of major changes in world commodity prices in the early 1930s and the devaluation of sterling in 1931 we clearly cannot attribute the fall in imports only to the effects of the General Tariff. However, there exists a *prima facie* case that the new policy *contributed* to these trends. Since the General Tariff had its greatest impact on manufacturing imports we need to consider whether tariffs had a significant effect on this component of demand. Kitson and Solomou (1990) test this by estimating an import function for UK manufacturing imports during the period 1924–38. Specifying the import function for UK manufactures as

$$M = a + b_1 Y + b_2 P + b_3 \tau + \varepsilon_t \qquad \ldots (1)$$

M = Manufacturing imports at constant prices
Y = Real GDP
P = Relative price of foreign to home manufactures
τ = ad valorem tariff rate

Specifying the import function in this general form explicitly considers the impact of the tariff, controlling for the effect of other important variables[2]. The results are presented in table 6.3. The fit gives an $\bar{R}_2$ value of 0.89. All the variables have the expected sign and the income and tariff coefficients are statistically significant at the 99 per cent confidence level. The relative price variable is significant at the 95 per cent level (one-tailed test). The results suggest that UK manufacturing imports were income elastic with an elasticity above 2. The tariff had a large depressing effect on import demand – a one percentage point increase in tariff rates resulted in a 3.4 percentage change in manufacturing imports. The relative price effect is significantly smaller (a 1 per cent change in relative prices gave rise to a 1.06 per cent change in manufactured imports).[3]

These results suggest that the impact of tariffs on import demand did not work through a simple price effect; the tariff effect was significantly higher than the non-tariff relative price effect. One interpretation may be that the tariff (because of its permanence) is capturing a long-run price elasticity of demand for imports which is significantly higher than the short-run elasticity. The results are also consistent with the view that tariffs had significant indirect effects on the demand for imports; to the extent that tariffs stimulated scale-intensive industries, the behaviour of pricing and production of such

[2] Given a proportional relationship between income and manufacturing imports the logarithmic specification of equation (1) is estimated. The only variable that is not expressed in logs is the tariff which is already expressed as a percentage rate.

[3] The restriction that the coefficients of log$P$ and τ are equal is rejected (Kitson and Solomou, 1990)

Table 6.3. OLS regression results for UK manufacturing import function, 1924–38 (t-values in parentheses)

Results of regressing:

$$\log M = \alpha + \beta_1 \log Y + \beta_2 \log P + \beta_3 \tau + \varepsilon_t$$

$\hat{\alpha}$	−6.772	−(1.83)	$\bar{R}^2 = 0.89$
β_1	2.114	(7.41)	$DW = 2.07$
β_2	−1.064	−(1.86)	$F = 37.02$
β_3	−0.034	−(10.30)	

Note: P relates to the lag of the relative price variable; the tariff rate used aims to capture the effect of the policy change in 1932 and takes the value of zero between 1924–31 and the manufacturing average tariff rate reported in Kitson and Solomou (1990), table A4.1 between 1932 and 1938.

industries had a significant indirect effect on import demand. The section on tariffs and scale intensive industries, below, considers the evidence for this effect.

IMPORT SUBSTITUTION

Given the degree of excess capacity in 1932, and the success of tariffs in reducing the demand for imports, protection is expected to generate a process of import substitution in production: the 'newly protected' industries of 1932 received a favourable stimulus, improving their standing relative to the non-protected and already protected industries. However, in an empirical evaluation of this hypothesis Richardson (1967, p. 249) concludes:

> The tariff had little effect on the growth of newly protected industries between 1930 and 1935.

This conclusion was based on Richardson's evaluation of the effects of protection on output, employment and trade in the newly protected industries of 1932 relative to those protected earlier. Richardson's argument is developed in two steps. The first simply compares the newly protected industries with other industries during the benchmark years 1930 and 1935 (the choice of these two years is determined by the available data: the censuses of production provide extensive disaggregated data). Richardson's results are presented in table 6.4. Given that between 1930 and 1935 the fall in imports in newly protected industries was less than the fall in imports of other industries, Richardson favours a non-tariff explanation for the healthy performance of the newly protected industries. Recovery in the newly protected sector was thus seen as simply reflecting general economic recovery in the 1930s. The second step of Richardson's evidence is based on calculating import replacement ratios for the newly protected and other industries between 1930 and 1935. The Import Replacement Ratio of an industry is defined as:

$$IRR = \frac{\text{rise in gross output} - \text{change in exports}}{\text{fall in imports}}$$

If a process of import substitution is observed in the 1930s then the fall in imports should lead to a proportional expansion of production for the home market (rise in gross output *minus* change in exports), assuming a constant level of demand. Thus, *ceteris paribus*, the ratio should tend to unity if import substitution is successful (a 1 per cent fall in imports should result in a 1 per cent increase in production for the home market). Given that the level of demand was not constant Richardson tests for the impact of the tariff by comparing the *relative* performance of the newly protected and other industries between 1930 and 1935: if the tariff succeeded in generating a process of import substitution then the IRR is expected to be closer to unity for the newly protected industries than for other industries. In fact the IRR takes the value of 3.0 for the newly protected industries and 2.0 for other industries (see table 6.4). From this evidence Richardson concludes that import substitution was not observed in the 1930s recovery.

A major weakness in Richardson's analysis is the implicit assumption that the newly protected and other industries begin from similar initial conditions in 1930. There is no attempt to compare the economic performance of the newly protected and other industries over a longer period that would allow us to test this assumption. The initial conditions in the 1920s will be unimportant only if industries were comparable in economic performance. We know this was not the case. The newly protected industries of 1932 consisted of many of the under-performing industries of the 1920s. The relevant question that Richardson's study does not address is the extent to which protection in 1932 reversed this path of decline. In order to evaluate this we need more information on the relative behaviour of the two groups of industries in the pre-protection period. Only by making such interperiod comparisons can we hope to test for the effects of policy changes.

The data contained in the Censuses of Production of 1924, 1930 and 1935 are at a sufficient level of disaggregation to allow us to distinguish the performance of the newly protected industries of 1932 relative to other industries. However, instead of comparing the relative position of the newly protected industries only for the years 1930 and 1935, we can use the benchmark comparisons of 1924, 1930 and 1935 as a way of capturing changes in relative performance in the light of the initial conditions faced by different industries before the policy shift in 1932. *Thus, the interperiod difference in performance between 1924–30 and 1930–5 is the relevant measure of the effects of protection on different industries* (table 6.5). The import duties of 1932 covered the majority of manufacturing industry, accounting for some 85 per cent of manufacturing output. The remaining industries had been protected under

Table 6.4. The effects of protection on industries newly protected in 1931–2 (total % change)

	Imports 1931–2	Imports 1930–5	Net output 1930–5	Employment 1930–5	Net output per head 1930–5	Import replacement ratio
Newly protected	−48	−39	+23	+3	+19	3.0
Other	−37	−44	+10	+2	+8	2.0
All manufacturing	−45	−41	+18	+3	+14	2.6

Source: Richardson (1967, table 20).

Table 6.5. Import and export annual growth rate for the newly protected and non-newly protected manufacturing sector (current prices)

		Newly protected	Non-newly protected
Imports			
	1924–30	+0.50	–1.35
	1930–5	–9.16	–7.76
Exports			
	1924–30	–7.92	+0.20
	1930–5	–5.11	–4.84

Source: Kitson and Solomou (1990, p. 76).

earlier legislation, including motor cars, scientific instruments and synthetic chemicals.

In order to test whether sectoral growth was stimulated by tariffs let us consider the relative performance of the newly protected industries with respect to output and productivity growth: output growth in the newly protected group of 1932 was stagnant between 1924 and 1930 whilst the other sector saw a respectable growth of 2.7 per cent per annum (see table 6.6). However, during 1930–5 there occurred a substantial turnaround as the newly protected group grew at 3.8 per cent per annum whilst the other industries grew at 2.3 per cent per annum. The impact of the policy shift on productivity growth was also favourable, as is shown in table 6.7.

The General Tariff of 1932 is correlated with a turnaround in the performance of UK manufacturing industries. Studies that have not managed to distinguish this effect have confused a number of very different economic processes. Comparing the newly protected industries of 1932 with the performance of other industries only in the 1930s (as Richardson has done) is

Table 6.6. Output indices for the newly protected and non-newly protected manufacturing sectors (1935=100)

	Newly protected	Non-newly protected
1924	83.22	76.13
1930	82.83	89.18
1935	100.00	100.00
Growth per annum (%)		
1924–30	−0.1	+2.7
1930–5	+3.8	+2.3

Source: Kitson and Solomou (1990, p. 77).

equivalent to describing the life cycle and business cycle behaviour of these industries. By taking a longer run comparison over 1924, 1930 and 1935 we can document the magnitude of *change* in the 1930s relative to the 1920s which is more likely to capture the impact of the protectionist policy regime.

TARIFFS AND SCALE INTENSIVE INDUSTRIES

The impact of trade policy will depend on the characteristics of the protected industries. Scale intensive industries showed a significant improvement in performance (see table 6.8). The interperiod comparisons between 1924–30 and 1930–5 show an annual growth rate improvement of 1.4 per cent. The comparison between the newly protected industries and others suggests that most of the improvement in the 1930s can be attributed to the newly protected industries. The interperiod comparison for the newly protected group shows an improvement of 2.9 per cent per annum compared with 0.2 per cent for the already protected industries. The gains of the protected

152

Table 6.7. Labour productivity indices for the newly protected and non-newly protected sectors

	Newly protected	Non-newly protected
1924	85.1	84.4
1930	87.4	93.0
1935	100.00	100.00
Growth per annum (%)		
1924–30	+0.45	+1.43
1930–5	+2.73	+1.46

Source: Kitson and Solomou (1990, p. 77).

sector were not limited to the scale intensive industries. The labour intensive textile sector also received a major stimulus in the 1930s (Kitson and Solomou, 1990; Matthews *et al.* 1982).

DISCRIMINATORY TRADE POLICY AND TRADE REGIONALISATION

One of the key features of trade policy in the 1930s was its discriminatory nature: trade agreements with Australia, Canada, India, New Zealand and South Africa at Ottawa in 1932 resulted in the establishment of Imperial Preference, making the tariffs of 1932 discriminatory against foreign countries. Such discriminatory trade policies are thought to have led to the regionalisation of UK trade into two major trading blocs – Empire and Foreign. The evidence presented in Glickman (1947) supports this proposition; non-Empire imports fell from 71 per cent in 1931 to 59.6 per cent in 1938 and UK exports to foreign countries declined from 56.3 to 50.1 per cent. However, a dichotomous classification of the structure of trade (Empire and Foreign) fails to consider the more widespread

153

Table 6.8. Output indices for scale intensive industries
(1935=100)

	Newly protected	Non-newly protected
1924	80.45	78.21
1930	83.84	88.87
1935	100.00	100.00
Growth per annum (%)		
1924–30	+0.7	+2.2
1930–5	+3.6	+2.4

Source: Kitson and Solomou (1990, p. 80).

implications of discriminatory trade policy during the 1930s. Moreover, the share of the Empire in UK trade also rose during 1870–1913; hence, the discriminatory trade policies of the 1930s cannot be assumed to have *caused* this particular regionalisation pattern. In order to shed more light on whether Imperial Preference accelerated these long-term patterns Kitson and Solomou (1991) classified UK trading partners into five major 'blocs':

- The British empire and commonwealth, who were favoured by Imperial Preference and devalued early with the UK
- The gold bloc economies who were faced with tariffs and a competitive devaluation disadvantage
- The major industrial competitors (Germany and America) who were mainly affected by the General tariff rather than UK devaluation
- The non-Empire countries who negotiated favourable trade agreements for manufacturing products and devalued early
- The rest of the world group, which is taken to include all countries not belonging to one of the above blocs

This broad classification has a number of advantages over Glickman's dichotomous (Empire–Foreign) classification. First, considering exchange rate zones means we can isolate a further important determinant of UK trading patterns. Secondly, the classification of foreign countries into trade agreement countries and others allows us to evaluate whether trade agreements stimulated trade both with the Empire and non-Empire countries participating in these trade diverting schemes. Finally, the category of the rest of the world is very important in that it consists of many small countries at a similar stage of economic development to the Empire countries. Thus, it may be possible to isolate the influence of patterns of world development on UK trading flows from the effects of discriminatory trade policy.

The share of imports from Empire countries rose very rapidly in the 1930s. However, within the 'foreign' category we observe differing patterns which imply that Imperial Preference cannot explain all of the observed increase in the share of Empire countries. The gain of the Empire countries was most with respect to the gold bloc economies, suggesting that the overvaluation of gold bloc currencies gave a further boost to trade with the Empire – in addition to the discrimination implied by Imperial Preference. In addition, despite the preferential arrangements organised with some non-Empire countries, import shares from these countries did not grow in the 1930s; thus, trade agreements, in themselves, did not necessarily successfully stimulate trade with preferential zones. Moreover, the rest of the world group raised its share of UK imports despite the adverse effects of discriminatory trade policies; thus, some of the increasing share of Empire countries have been due to similar factors that were giving rise to an increase in the share of imports from the rest of the world. However, the differences in the *magnitude* of the changes of the two groups show clearly that there was an Imperial Preference effect on the regional structure of UK trade in 1932–8.

Estimating the size of this effect is not as simple as Glickman (1947) implies. Only a proportion of the observed increase in the share of imports coming from the Empire resulted from the effects of Imperial Preference. Uncoordinated exchange rate policies, which put the gold bloc economies at a significant competitive disadvantage, and the import substitution strategies of a number of primary producing economies in the 1930s (such as Brazil) also affected the regionalisation of trade during this period.

Thus, the new discriminatory trade policy had significant effects on the regional distribution of UK trade. The macroeconomic effects of the new trading arrangements also need to be emphasised. Through such policies the UK was successful in creating a trading bloc that generated an expansion of trade that was superior to other blocs, such as those created by France and Germany (Eichengreen and Irwin, 1993). Although the increase was not of such a magnitude to account for the strength of the recovery in the 1930s, it contributed to the early stages of the cyclical recovery. However, we should also realise that the legacies of these policies survived into the postwar era. The UK saw Imperial Preference as a successful trading arrangement and held on to it, preventing a successful integration with Europe in the postwar era. Given that intra-European trade expanded so rapidly after the Second World War the UK's discriminatory trading arrangements appear to have been a constraint on the long-run expansion of trade.

CONCLUSIONS

The evidence that we have considered suggests that the General Tariff of 1932 succeeded in its aims of contributing to economic revival in the 1930s. This does not rule out the importance of other policies and 'natural' cyclical recovery factors (Kitson and Solomou, 1990). The following are the major conclusions that can be drawn from this chapter:

- A process of import substitution can be seen in the information contained in the Censuses of Production of 1924, 1930 and 1935.
- Industrial revival was reinforced by favourable macro-economic effects arising from the General Tariff: import propensities fell in the 1930s on a permanent basis, allowing the economy to expand to a higher level of domestic income than would have been possible otherwise. Without an explicit discussion of trade policy measures we cannot account for such import propensity changes.
- The price behaviour of the economy resulting from the effects of the General Tariff suggests that a competitive gain survived during the 1930s. This gain was largest in 1932–3 when tariffs were reinforced by the effects of a nominal exchange rate devaluation. Even if the two policies were contradictory in the long run, as Mundell's (flexible exchange rate) framework implies, the impact effect on the turning point from the depression and the early recovery period generated favourable effects on the output of scale intensive industries and a favourable effect on investment and output in the labour intensive industries. It is also unlikely that Mundell's assumptions of flexible prices and full employment provide a realistic basis for analysing the effects of the General Tariff during the 1930s.
- The analysis of this chapter has focused on the effects of protection on the cyclical recovery of the 1930s. We have not addressed the much broader question of whether protection in 1932 generated longer-term benefits for the UK economy. One could, in fact, argue convincingly that the protectionist regime of the 1930s imposed a longer-term constraint on the performance of the postwar economy (Broadberry and

Crafts, 1990). By stimulating a production structure that was based on the traditional staple industries, the necessary diversification of the UK economy was further delayed; thus, while the policy succeeded in contributing to cyclical recovery, a different response would have been needed to stimulate long-run economic growth.

• The new trade regionalisation contributed to economic recovery in the 1930s. However, the new trading arrangements were persistent, surviving into the postwar period. Under new conditions in the postwar era the interwar arrangements became a constraint to the expansion of trade; by fostering trade with the Empire the UK missed out on the rapid growth of intra-European trade during the golden age of the postwar era.

SELECTED FURTHER READING

Broadberry, S.N. (1986) *The British Economy Between the Wars*, (chapter 13).

Capie, F. (1978) 'The British Tariff and Industrial Protection in the 1930s', *Economic History Review*.

Capie, F. (1994) *Tariffs and Growth: Some Insights From the World Economy, 1850–1940*.

Foreman-Peck, J. S. (1981) 'The British Tariff and Industrial Protection in the 1930s: An Alternative Model', *Economic History Review*.

Kitson, M. and Solomou, S.N, (1990) *Protectionism and Economic Revival: The British Interwar Economy*.

Kitson, M., Solomou S.N. and Weale M. (1991) 'Effective Protection and Economic Recovery in the United Kingdom During the 1930s', *Economic History Review*.

Richardson, H.W. *Economic Recovery in Britain, 1932–9*, (chapter 10).

CHAPTER 7

POLICY LESSONS OF THE INTERWAR PERIOD

INTRODUCTION

This chapter focuses on a selection of policy issues that were important to contemporaries of the period and remain on the policy agenda today. The interwar experience of diverse exchange rate regimes, protectionism, mass unemployment, poor long-run economic growth, disintegrating world trade and high business cycle volatility makes the period extremely interesting to policy-makers. The objectivity of historical lessons, however, needs to be placed in the context of the interests of policy-makers. Their attempts at instituting change may result in interpretations of the past that are misleading as universal policy lessons. To illustrate the nature of this problem we should note that recent historical research has completely reversed many of the interpretations made by economists in the early postwar period. For example, postwar policy-makers used the interwar experience to draw the lesson that high costs are incurred when fixed exchange rates are allowed to collapse. The League of Nations (Nurkse, 1944) suggested that the period of devaluation and protectionism during the 1930s left all nations worse off. There is now extensive evidence, however, that the gold exchange standard that operated in the 1920s was far from ideal. The system was maladjusted in the sense that it operated around an asymmetric

159

adjustment mechanism, with only deficit countries having to generate adjustment in response to balance of payments problems; surplus countries continued to maintain their surpluses during 1925–33 (Temin,1989; Eichengreen, 1992; Kitson and Michie, 1994). Breaking from this system allowed the UK economy to benefit from expansionary non-inflationary policies in the 1930s. This example illustrates how the lessons of history evolve in the light of new evidence about the past and new policy debates that encourage economic historians and policy-makers to reevaluate the foundations of old facts.

LESSON 1: IS TRADE PROTECTION POLICY NECESSARILY BAD?

Postwar policy-makers created the foundations of a new international economic order around a number of beliefs about interwar trade policy: protection and depression were seen to be inextricably related in a causal manner, as was protection and the disintegration of world trade. This view continues to find support today (Capie, 1992; Capie, 1994). However, the picture of interwar protection that is emerging in recent research is far more complex: some countries gained, others lost (Kitson and Solomou, 1990); some trading blocs were able to expand trade in the adverse circumstances of the 1930s, others were not successful (Eichengreen and Irwin, 1993).

In order to understand why countries chose the protectionist path in the early 1930s it is not sufficient simply to argue that protection policies were an outcome of interest group policies that did not serve countries well. We need to understand the historical context of these type of policies. Two key features need to be emphasised: first, the 1930s was a period when existing institutions were failing to generate high employment and output levels; secondly, the policy framework was still very much based on *national* decision-making. Protection policy offered an appropriate national response to external shocks. It is misleading simply to point to the lost opportunities that accompanied the abandonment of free trade. Countries had the choice of raising interest rates and deflating further to control their worsening balance of payments problems or to protect. Protection offered a viable national-specific policy option. This was particularly true for the UK which had pursued a *unilateral* free trade strategy up to the 1930s. Continuing with unilateral free trade, in the unique circumstances of world depression during the 1930s would have cost Britain dearly in terms of output and unemployment.

This picture differs from that drawn by policy-makers in the early postwar period. To reconcile these differing views it is important to realise that postwar policy-makers were attempting to build the foundations for a New Economic Order by creating institutions that were going to restabilise the world economy in the long run (such as GATT): a qualified evaluation of the protectionist measures adopted during the interwar era would not have been a politically viable way of generating institutional change. However, one important function of historical analysis is to identify the complexities of actual policy choices. As it turned out the shocks of the post-1973 era have led to a resurgence of protectionist measures and regional trade policies that look like a repeat of the 1930s experience. This recurrence should guide us towards a reevaluation of the underlying features of the interwar era that led to a wave of protectionism. The underlying conditions behind interwar protectionism were:

• large asymmetric shocks across countries
• a lack of international policy coordination
• national-specific policy pressures

Although it is unlikely that governments can influence the distribution of shocks, they can influence the degree of international and regional policy coordination. The formation of a number of trading and possibly macroeconomic policy blocs may mean that the world economy can avoid national-specific protection measures today. However, at the international level, it would be ahistorical to argue that particular regions should learn from the experience of the 1930s and avoid protection at all costs: this must be a function of the nature of shocks and the nature of the adjustments that are possible (including the degree of international policy coordination). Judged in this context the protectionism of the UK during the 1930s was a rational response to shocks in the light of specific historical circumstances that determined policy options. Pointing out that a different mix of institutions can result in improved economic performance may be sobering but anachronistic.

LESSON 2: FIXED OR FLEXIBLE EXCHANGE RATES?

The interwar period witnessed a diversity of exchange rate regimes (flexible, 1919–25; fixed, 1925–31; managed, 1931–39). Comparisons across these different eras have been used to analyse the relative performance of different exchange rate regimes. Great care needs to be exercised when making such comparisons. For example, the period 1919–25 is often seen as one of the few examples of a flexible exchange rate regime. However, although in technical terms the exchange rate was flexible, in that *direct* government intervention in the exchange rate market was limited, the period is not a good example of how a flexible exchange rate system works as an overall policy regime. As early as 1919 (the same year as the exit from the gold standard) the UK government had committed itself to the reestablishment of the fixed pre-war gold parity. Hence, the observed volatility of nominal and real economic variables during the flexible exchange rate era is, partly, the outcome of an announced transition period to fixed exchange rates. The macroeconomic policy stance of the period 1919–25 was one that attempted to *switch* exchange rate regimes. This switching, as we have seen above, had significant costs of adjustment; to see this era as a straightforward example of a flexible exchange rate regime is to miss the point.

The workings of the gold exchange system during 1925–31 are also complex and should not be taken as a simple example of the way fixed exchange rate regimes function. The inability of the world economic system to generate a viable symmetric adjustment mechanism for surplus and deficit countries shows that a maladjusted system has high costs in terms of output and unemployment. The collapse of this system in the 1930s should not be seen as a policy mistake. Countries were forced into a situation where they needed to introduce some changes to a malfunctioning system. Since the world economic system was not sufficiently coordinated to generate an international response to economic problems, national specific policies provided the only realistic policy options. To the extent that each of the national specific moves of the 1930s lacked coordination they were not optimal policy responses; however, the devaluations of the 1930s created an opportunity for some fresh evolution from a system that was becoming a serious constraint to the smooth functioning of the world economy (Eichengreen, 1992). The main lesson to be drawn from this example is that the functioning of an exchange rate regime needs to be evaluated in the context of changing historical circumstances: the changes observed in the interwar period meant that fixed exchange rates ended up being a serious constraint to price stability and economic growth.

LESSON 3: CAN FISCAL POLICY WORK?

Postwar Keynesian perspectives to economic policy management looked back to the interwar experience of mass unemployment and depressed output and argued the need for government fiscal policy to stabilise the economy. The emphasis on fiscal policy (as against monetary policy) partly reflected the acceptance of a fixed exchange rate institutional framework, which limited the use of an activist monetary policy.

Our survey of specific interwar problems qualifies the feasibility of fiscal policy as an instrument for economic adjustment to adverse shocks. The shocks of the early 1920s were partly the outcome of the overall policy choices; in particular the choice of returning to the gold standard at the pre-1913 gold parity. Fiscal policy will only be useful as a tool to manage demand if the government has chosen an institutional structure which provides a viable framework for sustainable economic growth. Similarly, the argument that fiscal policy should have been used to solve the problems of the Great Depression fails to recognise that one important 'shock' behind the depression was the contractionary policies resulting from the defence of the gold standard. The use of fiscal policy within the existing institutional framework would have been self-defeating because expansionary fiscal policy would have been seen to be in conflict with the sustainability of the gold standard. Both examples serve to show that the use of fiscal policy is not independent of other policy choices.

LESSON 4: 'HISTORY MATTERS'

Increasingly economists and economic historians have recognised the importance of historical events and policies in determining the 'equilibrium' paths that economies follow. It is in this sense that we use the phrase 'history matters'. This theoretical stance is in marked contrast to the recent New-Classical models of the economy that see policy (at least demand side policy) as having only *transitory* effects.

Three examples will serve to illustrate the relevance of this point. First, our evaluation of the immediate post-First World War depression showed that transitory shocks during 1919–21 resulted in a permanent effect on the capacity level of the economy, as measured by high unemployment rates and a low output level. Second, the policy regime shifts of the early 1930s (devaluation, protection, cheap money) served the purpose of reducing the permanent damage of going through a longer depression. Thus, devaluation in 1931 prevented a deeper depression in the UK compared to the late devaluers (Eichengreen, 1992). Finally, the path of unemployment can only be understood in the context of specific shocks. For example, the creation of long-term unemployment in the 1930s is the result of transitory shocks that had persistent effects.

The general policy implication of these examples is that the distinction between short-run and long-run policy goals is highly blurred. Governments cannot hold to the view that in the long run the effects of policy mistakes are averaged out. Major policy mistakes can leave permanent scars.

SELECTED FURTHER READING

Capie, F. (1992), 'Trade Wars: A Repetition of the Interwar Years?', Institute of Economic Affairs.

Cooper, R.N. (1992), 'Fettered on Gold? Economic Policies in the Interwar Period', *Journal of Economic Literature*.

Eichengreen, B. (1992), *Golden Fetters: The Gold Standard and the Great Depression 1919–1939*.

Kitson, M. and Michie, J. (1994), 'Co-ordinated Deflation – The Tale of Two Recessions', in Michie, J. and Grieve Smith, J. (eds.), *Unemployment in Europe*.

Nurkse, R. (1944), *International Currency Experience*.

Temin, P. (1989), *Lessons From the Great Depression*.

GLOSSARY

AD VALOREM TARIFF

A tax imposed on particular imports as a percentage of value. For example, the 1932 ad valorem rate was 10 per cent. An alternative way of imposing a tariff is on a specific basis (a fixed amount per unit imported).

ACCELERATOR THEORY

This is a theory of investment determination. The simple 'naive' accelerator models the level of investment as being determined by the change in aggregate output or consumption,

$$I_t = v(Y_t - Y_{t-1}) = v(\Delta Y_t)$$
$$I_t = v(C_t - C_{t-1}) = v(\Delta C_t)$$

I_t = level of investment
Y_t = level of output
C_t = level of expenditure on consumption goods
v = constant

This relationship is often specified as a linear relationship, where the parameter v is constant. However, in business cycle discussions it is recognised that non-linear specifications may be more realistic. For example, at high levels of output change we may not observe rising investment because of capacity constraints in the capital producing sector.

166

GLOSSARY

AMPLITUDE

Measures the variance of the business cycle. One simple measure is to take the peak to trough variations over the business cycle.

AUCTION MARKET

A market where demand and supply conditions determine the equilibrium price-quantity outcomes.

BANK RATE

The interest rate charged by the Bank of England to other banks. This will, in turn, influence market interest rates as banks adjust their interest rates.

BILATERAL EXCHANGE RATE

The rate at which one currency is exchanged for another. For example, the 1913 rate between the dollar and the pound was 4.86 dollars to the pound. A further distinction needs to be made between the spot rate and the forward rate. In the interwar period a forward exchange market operated for one month or three month forward purchases; market expectations determined a premium or a discount to the spot rate. See also Multilateral exchange rate.

BRETTON WOODS

The international agreement resulting from the 1944 conference held at Bretton Woods (USA) to discuss alternative proposals from the US, UK and Canada. The agreement set up the International Monetary Fund and the World Bank. The two key aims of these new institutions were stable exchange rates and the provision of sufficient finance for postwar reconstruction.

GLOSSARY

CAPITAL–OUTPUT RATIO

This measures the stock of capital in the economy relative to the *flow* of aggregate output (GDP) in any one year. The ratio can be measured in either constant or current prices.

CO-INTEGRATED VARIABLES

Two series that are non-stationary may be co-integrated if a linear combination of the two time series is stationary. For this to arise the two variables must share common trends, rising and falling jointly.

COMPARATIVE ADVANTAGE

A country is said to have comparative advantage in producing a particular good if its relative costs of production for the good are lower than other countries.

CONSOLS

This is an abbreviation for consolidated stock. They are an irredeemable government stock and bear a fixed interest rate. Being irredeemable means the owner is entitled to interest payments but not to a repaymant of the face value of the capital. Thus the market price for the consol will vary. The consol rate is often used as a measure of long-term market interest rates.

CROWDING OUT

The processes by which government actions may reduce private expenditures. For example, a fiscal policy that raises interest rates will reduce private sector interest sensitive expenditures. Similarly a contractionary monetary policy that results in an appreciation of the exchange rate will adversely affect the tradable sector.

CYCLICAL UNEMPLOYMENT

Unemployment variations resulting from business cycle fluctuations. It has been conventional to decompose unemployment into separate structural, cyclical and frictional components.

'DEAD-WEIGHT LOSS'

A tariff distorts domestic consumption and production relative to the free trade scenario. Tariffs reduce the consumption of imported goods and force up domestic prices. Although producers gain from the rise in domestic prices there occurs a net loss to society – often referred to as a 'dead-weight loss'.

EFFECTIVE EXCHANGE RATE

See multilateral exchange rate.

ELASTICITY

A unit free measure relating the percentage change of one variable to another. For example the price elasticity of demand relates the percentage change of the price of a good to the percentage change in demand.

EXCHANGE EQUALISATION ACCOUNT

This was a foreign exchange account (set up by the Finance Act of 1932) controlled by the Treasury and managed by the Bank of England with the aim of stabilising the value of the pound against other major currencies. France and America operated a similar scheme in the 1930s.

EXOGENOUS

Refers to that which is caused outside a specific system being analysed. For example, as economists we typically take the political system and psychological attitudes as given.

FUNDAMENTAL EQUILIBRIUM EXCHANGE RATE

That exchange rate which permits a long-run sustainable balance of payments position which is consistent with full utilisation of resources and stable inflation.

GATT

General Agreement on Tariffs and Trade signed at Bretton Woods in 1946 to reduce tariff and non-tariff barriers to trade and to encourage an end of the discriminatory trade arrangements of the 1930s. There have been a number of GATT negotiated agreements since then that have attempted to reduce trade barriers further and to encourage the conduct of multilateral trade.

GOLD EXCHANGE STANDARD

A system of international payments which values currencies at fixed amounts of gold or of other currencies fixed to gold. Under this system paper currency was not convertible into gold but into the currency of some other country on the gold standard. A gold exchange standard was operating during 1925–31 with the dollar playing an important role as a reserve currency.

GOLD STANDARD

A system of international payments which values currencies at fixed amounts of gold. All the major industrial counties (Britain, France, Germany and USA) operated a gold standard during 1879–1914. However, even during this period a gold exchange standard was evolving with sterling increasingly acting as reserve currency.

GROSS DOMESTIC PRODUCT DEFLATOR

A price index used to deflate the nominal value of goods and services produced in a particular country. In practice the GDP deflator is derived as an implicit deflator by dividing the value measure of GDP with the volume measure.

HUMAN CAPITAL
A measure of the stock of knowledge accumulated over time.

HYSTERESIS
Transitory shocks have permanent effects on the equilibrium path of a variable (see also non-stationary variables). As an example, unemployment may display the phenomenon of hysteresis if during major depressions workers become unemployed for long durations, leading to an atrophy of human capital and a permanent rise in long-term unemployment levels.

'IDENTIFICATION PROBLEM'
Whenever statistical relationships are simultaneously determined, an identification problem arises. For example, both demand and supply are a function of price. Hence, observing data for prices and output is not sufficient to determine whether we are observing a demand curve or a supply curve. To identify these relationships we need to explicitly model demand and supply relationships simultaneously.

IMF
International Monetary Fund: founded at Bretton Woods in 1944 to provide short-term finance for member countries participating in the fixed exchange rate regime, allowing them to cope with temporary balance of payments problems.

IMPORT (PENETRATION) RATIO
The share of imports in domestic expenditure. The aggregate import ratio can be defined as total imports as a share of GDP (which can be measured in either value or volume terms).

INCREASING RETURNS TO SCALE

If all inputs in a production function are increased by some proportion (say 10 per cent) and output increased by more than 10 per cent the returns to scale are said to be increasing. If output expands by exactly 10 per cent, returns to scale are constant. If output increases by less than 10 per cent returns to scale are decreasing.

INTER-TEMPORAL DECISIONS

Decisions made in one time period that take into account expectations about the future.

INTRA-INDUSTRY TRADE

This refers to the trade of similar commodities across countries (for example, British cars traded for Japanese cars). The twentieth century has seen an expansion of intra-industry trade which is also reflected in new regional trading patterns (for example, intra-European trade has expanded rapidly).

JUGLAR CYCLE

A trade cycle of eight to nine years duration. The cycle is named after Clement Juglar who was one of the first trade cycle researchers to observe this periodicity in the nineteenth century.

KONDRATIEFF WAVE

A cycle of prices and output with an approximate periodicity of 50 to 60 years. The 'upswing' of the cycle represents a phase of rapid economic growth lasting between 20 and 30 years; the 'downswing' of the cycle shows a retardation in economic growth of a similar duration.

KUZNETS SWING

A cycle in economic growth that is approximately twenty years in duration. The actual length of the swings found varies with

172

different authors, but something between 14 and 22 years is representative. This cycle is named after Simon Kuznets who was one of the first economists to observe the phenomenon.

LABOUR HOARDING

Refers to the view that firms retain excess labour during recessions, with the expectation of utilising the excess labour during the recovery period.

LABOUR PRODUCTIVITY

Output per unit of labour input. Labour input can either be measured in hours worked or number of workers.

MCKENNA DUTIES

Import tariffs on cars, films and other luxury products imposed by the Chancellor of the Exchequer in 1915 as an emergency wartime measure to save shipping space. Although seen as a temporary measure when they were introduced, they were not removed after the war.

MONOPOLISTIC COMPETITION

Refers to a market structure where there is a large number of firms producing differentiated products. Product differentiation means that a particular firm can raise its price without losing all its market share. Hence, product differentiation means that the demand curve is downward sloping rather than horizontal as in the theory of perfect competition.

MULTILATERAL EXCHANGE RATE

An index of exchange rates relating one currency to a basket of other currencies. The weights for constructing the basket can either be taken from bilateral trade shares or shares of world trade. Using bilateral trade shares captures the strength of bilateral trade flows, while shares of world trade capture the fact that countries with weak direct trade may be significant competitors in 'third markets'.

NATURAL GROWTH

The maximal growth rate made possible by the expansion of the labour force and technical progress.

NON-TREND-STATIONARY

If the movement of a variable, once shocked away from equilibrium, does not revert back to a well-defined trend value it is said to be non-trend-stationary. The variable tends to drift away from a mean value.

PARTICIPATION RATIO

The percentage of a specified population who work in the market economy. For example, the participation ratio for women is the per cent of women aged 16–60 who work in the market economy. The lower and upper age bands are determined by the legal requirements of education and retirement.

PRIMARY PRODUCERS

Refers to countries or sectors within a country with a trade and production specialisation that is concentrated in agricultural or raw material commodities.

PRO-CYCLICAL MOVEMENTS

If variables move in the same direction over the business cycle we describe their relationship as pro-cyclical. For example, real wages move pro-cyclically with employment if real wage increases are associated with rising employment. If variables move inversely over the business cycle their relationship is described as contra-cyclical.

PURCHASING POWER PARITY (PPP) THEORY

This is a theory of exchange rate determination. It can either be expressed in an 'absolute' or 'relative' specification. The simplest version of the absolute theory is the law of one price, which means that arbitrage across countries will result in the price of goods being equal across countries. Aggregating across goods this can be expressed as,

$$P = eP*$$

P = domestic price level
$P*$ = foreign price level

Hence, the exchange rate (e) can be expressed as the ratio of foreign and domestic price levels. The relative version was developed by Gustav Cassel in his analysis of the flexible exchange rate experience of 1919–25. In this theory exchange rate changes reflect inflationary shocks to different countries. Thus, if a national specific monetary shock leads to inflation at home this will result in a depreciated exchange rate.

RANDOM WALK

This describes the path of a variable over time in which successive values are independent. At any point in time there are n possible moves which are all equally probable. The specific move that occurs is dependent on the nature of historical shocks.

REAL INTEREST RATES

The real interest rate can be defined as the nominal interest rate minus the rate of inflation. For example, if the nominal interest rate is 10 per cent and the expected inflation rate is 8 per cent, the real interest rate is 2 per cent.

REAL WAGES

Nominal wages deflated by a relevant price index. Deflating nominal wages by a retail price index gives us a measure of consumption real wages; deflating by the gross domestic product deflator gives us a measure of product real wages faced by employers.

RECONSTRUCTION PERIOD

Refers to the catch-up growth observed after major events such as war. The reconstruction period after the First World War can be split into the early post-war phase of 1918–24 and the more stable phase during the late 1920s (1924–9).

RETAINED IMPORTS

Total imports minus re-exports. This latter category consists of goods on sale on the commodity markets which do not leave customs until exported.

'SECOND-BEST THEORY'

This theory, developed by Lipsey and Lancaster, argues that if there exists some distortion in the economy preventing a perfectly competitive equilibrium (such as a monopoly in one sector) it would not be optimal for the remaining sectors to attain the perfectly competitive equilibrium. Optimality requires that the remaining sectors adopt a position that diverges from the perfectly competitive equilibrium. Applied to international trade theory, if some countries protect their home markets it will not be in the interest of the world economy for the others to pursue unilateral free trade strategies (unless their example encourages the protected economies to move to a free trade stance).

SEGMENTED TREND

If long-run time series data contain a break in trend we can describe the long-run movements as a segmented trend. The number of segments depends on the number of breaks in the data.

176

GLOSSARY

STAPLE SECTORS

Refers to the key traditional industries accounting for a high proportion of total UK industrial output. These were textiles, iron and steel, coal and shipbuilding. Although there was some diversification of the industrial structure during the interwar period these industries continued to be the largest industries.

STERLING BLOC

When the pound left the gold standard in September 1931 a large number of Empire and non-Empire countries linked their currencies to the British pound (sterling). This grouping is often referred to as the sterling area. In 1939 this arrangement was formalised with the acceptance of exchange controls in respect of transactions with non-sterling area countries.

'TARIFF JUMPING'

This refers to a situation where a tariff encourages foreign firms to undertake direct investment in the country imposing a tariff. By setting up production in the protected country the firm can avoid paying the tariff.

TERMS OF TRADE

The ratio of export prices to import prices (often referred to as the net barter terms of trade). If export prices rise faster than import prices (or alternatively, fall more slowly than import prices) the terms of trade are said to 'improve'. The *gross terms of trade* measure changes in the quantity relationship of exports and imports.

TRANSITORY (RANDOM) SHOCK

A short-term shock to a variable. For example, an appreciation of the exchange rate will induce a transitory shock to the economy if the appreciation is, on average, followed by depreciation. Whether a transitory shock results in transitory or permanent effects depends on whether the history of the shock is important to the new equilibrium. For example, if a random shock to the exchange rate (leading to a domestic appreciation) encourages foreign firms to set up production and distribution networks they may choose to remain in the new market even though the exchange rate moves against them in future periods.

TRANS-WAR PERIOD
The period 1913–24 has often been referred to as the 'trans-war years' (Matthews *et al.*, 1982). The choice of 1924 as the endpoint results from the idea that the reconstruction period from the First World War was sufficient to allow the economy to return to a comparable level of activity to that observed in 1913.

TREND-STATIONARY SERIES
Describes a time series which follows a well-defined trend value. In the long-run upward deviations will be followed by downward deviations. In this sense transitory shocks have transitory effects on the specific variable.

UNIT LABOUR COSTS
Measures labour costs per unit of output. The path of unit labour costs will vary positively with nominal wages and negatively with productivity growth.

WAGE-GAP
Relates the growth rate of real wages to that of labour productivity. A wage gap will arise if real-wage growth is in excess of productivity growth.

BIBLIOGRAPHY

Abramovitz, M. (1968), 'The Passing of the Kuznets Cycle', *Economica*, 35: 349–67.

Aldcroft, D.H. (1967), 'Economic Growth in Britain in the Interwar Years: A Reassessment', *Economic History Review*, 20: 311–26.

(1986a), *The British Economy*, vol. I, Wheatsheaf, Brighton.

(1986b), 'Great Britain – The Constraints to Full Employment in the 1930s and 1980s', in Berend, I. and Borchardt, K. (eds.), *The Impact of the Depression in the 1930s and Its Relevance for the Contemporary World*, Karl Marx University of Economics, Budapest.

Aldcroft, D.H. and Fearon, P. (eds.) (1969), *Economic Growth in 20th Century Britain*, Macmillan, London.

Alford, B.W.E. (1972), *Depression and Recovery? British Economic Growth, 1918–1939*, Macmillan, London.

Andrews, B.P. (1982), 'The UK Exchange Rate in the 1920s', unpublished, Oxford.

Arndt, H.W. (1944), *The Economic Lessons of the 1930s*, Oxford University Press for the Royal Institute of International Affairs, Oxford.

Backus, D.K. and Kehoe, P.J. (1992), 'International Evidence on the Historical Properties of Business Cycles', *American Economic Review*, 82, 4: 864–88.

Bairoch, P. (1986), 'Commercial Policies and Economic Development in History: Myth and Reality of Protectionism', *Journal of Regional Policy*, 4, 86: 512–34.

Balassa, B. (1964), 'The Purchasing Power Parity Doctrine: A Reappraisal', *Journal of Political Economy*, 72: 584–96.

179

Barna, T. (1952), 'The Interdependence of the British Economy', *Journal of the Royal Statistical Society*, series A: 29–77.

Barro R.J. (1981), *Money, Expectations and Business Cycles*, New York.

Barro, R.J and Grossman, H.I. (1971): 'A General Disequilibrium Model of Income and Employment', *American Economic Review*, 61: 82–93.

Beenstock, M. and Warburton, P. (1983), 'Long-Term Trends in Economic Openness in the United Kingdom and the United States', *Oxford Economic Papers*, 35: 130–40.

(1986), 'Wages and Unemployment in Interwar Britain', *Explorations in Economic History*, 23: 153–72.

Beenstock M. *et al.* (1984), 'Economic Recovery in the UK in the 1930s', Bank of England Panel Paper 23: 57–85.

Benjamin, D.K. and Kochin, L.A. (1979), 'Searching for an Explanation of Unemployment in Interwar Britain', *Journal of Political Economy*, 87: 441–70.

Bernake, B. and James, H. (1991), 'The Gold Standard, Deflation and Financial Crisis in the Great Depression: An International Comparison', in Hubbard, R.G. (ed.), *Financial Crisis*, Chicago.

Beveridge, W.H. (1944), *Full Employment in a Free Society*, London.

Blanchard, O.J. and Summers, L.H. (1986), 'Hysteresis and the European Unemployment Problem', in Fischer, S. (ed.), *NBER Macroeconomics Annual*, Cambridge, Mass.

Booth, A. and Glynn, S. (1975), 'Unemployment in the Interwar Period: A Multiple Problem', *Journal of Contemporary History*, 10: 611–36.

Bowden, S.M. (1988), 'The Consumer Durables Revolution in England, 1932-1938: A Regional Analysis', *Explorations in Economic History*, 25: 42–59.

Broadberry, S.N. (1983), 'Unemployment in Inter-war Britain: A Disequilibrium Approach', *Oxford Economic Papers*, 35: 463–85.

(1984), 'The North European Depression in the 1920s', *Scandinavian Economic History Review*, 32, 3: 159–67.

(1986), *The British Economy Between the Wars: A Macroeconomic Survey*, Basil Blackwell, Oxford.

(1987), 'Cheap Money and the Housing Boom in Interwar Britain: An Econometric Appraisal', *The Manchester School*, 87: 378–91.

(1990), 'The Emergence of Mass Unemployment: Explaining Macroeconomic Trends in Britain During the Trans-War Period', *Economic*

History Review, 43: 271–82.

Broadberry, S.N. and Crafts, N.F.R. (1990), 'The Impact of the Depression of the 1930s on the Production Potential of the United Kingdom', *European Economic Review*, 34: 599–607.

Butlin, N. and Gregory, R.G. (eds.) (1988), *Recovery from the Depression: Australia and the World Economy in the 1930s*, Cambridge.

Buxton, N.K. (1975), 'The Role of the "New Industries" in Britain During the 1930s: A Reinterpretation', *Business History Review*, 49: 205–22.

Cairncross, A.K. and Eichengreen, B.J. (1983), *Sterling in Decline*, Basil Blackwell, Oxford.

Capie, F. (1978), 'The British Tariff and Industrial Protection in the 1930s', *Economic History Review*, 31: 399–409.

(1980), 'The Pressure for Tariff Protection in Britain, 1917–31', *Journal of European Economic History*, 2: 431–48.

(1981), 'Tariffs, Elasticities and Prices in Britain in the 1930s', *Economic History Review*, 34, 1: 140–2.

(1983), *Depression and Protectionism: Britain Between the Wars*, George Allen & Unwin, London.

(1990), 'Money and Business Cycles in Britain 1870–1913', in Velupellai, N. and Thygesen, N. (eds.), *Business Cycles, Non Linearities, Disequilibrium, and Simulations: Readings in Business Cycles Theory*, London.

(1992), 'Trade Wars: A Repetition of the Interwar Years', IEA Paper, London.

(1994), *Tariffs and Growth: Some Insights From the World Economy, 1850-1940*, Manchester University Press, Manchester.

Capie, F. and Collins, M. (1980), 'The Extent of British Recovery in the 1930s', *Economy and History*, 23, 1: 40–60.

(1983), *The Interwar Economy: A Statistical Abstract*, Manchester University Press, Manchester.

Capie, F. and Mills, T.C. (1991), 'Money and Business Cycles in the US and UK, 1870 to 1913', *The Manchester School*, 53 (Supplement): 38–56.

Capie, F. and Webber, A. (1985), *A Monetary History of the United Kingdom, 1870-1982, Vol. I: Data, Sources, Methods*, Allen & Unwin, London.

Capie, F. and Wood, G. (1994), 'Money in the Economy, 1870–1939', in

181

Floud, R. and McCloskey, D.N. (eds.), The Economic History of Britain Since 1700, second edition.

Casson, M. (1983), *Economics of Unemployment: An Historical Perspective*, Martin Robertson, Oxford.

Catao, L.A.V. and Solomou, S.N. (1993), 'Business Cycles During the Gold Standard', Department of Applied Economics, Working Paper No. 9304, Cambridge University,

Choudri, E. and Kochin, L.A. (1980), 'The Exchange Rate and the International Transmission of Business Cycle Disturbances', *Journal of Money, Credit and Banking*, 12, 4: 565–74.

Collins, M. (1982), 'Unemployment in Interwar Britain: Still Searching for an Explanation', *Journal of Political Economy*, 90: 369–79.

Cooper, R.N. (1992), 'Fettered on Gold? Economic Policies in the Interwar Period', *Journal of Economic Literature*, 2120–8.

Corner, D.C. (1956), 'British Exports and the British Trade Cycle: 1929', *The Manchester School*, 24: 124–60.

Crafts, N.F.R. (1985), *British Economic Growth During the Industrial Revolution*, Oxford University Press, Oxford.

(1987), 'Long-Term Unemployment in Britain in the 1930s', *Economic History Review*, 40, 3: 418–32.

(1989), 'Long-Term Unemployment and the Wage Equation in Britain 1925–1939', *Economica*, 56: 247–54.

Crafts, N.F.R. and Thomas, M. (1986), 'Comparative Advantage in UK Manufacturing Trade, 1910–1935', *Economic Journal*, 96: 629–45.

Crafts, N.F.R, Leybourne, S.J. and Mills, T.C. (1989), 'The Climacteric in Late Victorian Britain and France: A Reappraisal of the Evidence', *Journal of Applied Econometrics*, 4: 103–17.

Dimsdale, N.H. (1981), 'British Monetary Policy and the Exchange Rate 1920–1938', in Eltis, W.A. and Sinclair, P.J.N. (eds.), *The Money Supply and the Exchange Rate*, Oxford University Press, Oxford.

(1984), 'Employment and Real Wages in the Inter-war period', *National Institute Economic Review*, 110: 94–103.

Dimsdale, N.H, Nickell, S.J. and Horsewood, N. (1989), 'Real Wages and Unemployment in Britain During the 1930s', *Economic Journal*, 99, 396: 271–92.

Dornbusch, R. (1976), 'Expectations and Exchange Rate Dynamics', *Journal of Political Economy*, 84: 1161–76.

Dowie, J. (1968), 'Growth in the Interwar Period: Some More Arithmetic',

Economic History Review, 21: 93–112.

(1975), '1919-20 is in Need of Attention', *Economic History Review*, 28: 429–50.

Drummond, I.M. (1981), *The Floating Pound and the Sterling Area, 1931–1939*, Cambridge University Press, Cambridge.

Dunlop, J.T. (1938), 'The Movement of Real and Money Wage Rates', *Economic Journal*, 48: 413–34.

Eichengreen, B.J. (1981), 'Sterling and the Tariff, 1929–32', *Princeton Studies in International Finance*, 48.

(1986), 'Understanding 1921–1927: Inflation and Economic Recovery in the 1920s', *Rivista di Storia Economica*, New Series, 5: 34–66.

(1987), 'Unemployment in Interwar Britain: Dole or Doldrums?' *Oxford Economic Papers*, 39: 597–623.

(1989), 'The Political Economy of the Smoot Hawley Tariff', *Research in Economic History*, 11: 1–44.

(1991), 'Relaxing the External Constraint: Europe in the 1930s', in Alogoskoufis, G., Papademos, L. and Portes, R. (eds.), *External Constraints on Macroeconomic Policy: The European Experience*, Cambridge.

(1992), *Golden Fetters: The Gold Standard and the Great Depression, 1919–1939*, Oxford.

(1994), 'The Inter-War Economy in a European Mirror', in Floud, R. and McCloskey, D.N., *The Economic History of Britain Since 1700*, second edition.

Eichengreen, B.J. and Hatton, T.J. (eds.) (1988), *Interwar Unemployment in International Perspective*, Martinus-Nijhoff, Dordrecht and Boston.

Eichengreen, B.J. and Irwin, D.A. (1993), 'Trade Blocs, Currency Blocs and the Disintegration of World Trade in the 1930s', mimeo.

Eichengreen, B.J. and Sachs, J. (1985), 'Exchange Rates and Economic Recovery in the 1930s', *Journal of Economic History*, 45: 925–46.

Feinstein, C.H. (1972), *National Income, Expenditure and Output of the United Kingdom, 1855–1965*, Cambridge University Press, Cambridge.

(1990), 'New Estimates of Average Earnings in the United Kingdom, 1880–1913', *Economic History Review*, 43: 595–632.

(1990), 'What Really Happened to Real Wages, Prices, and Productivity in the United Kingdom, 1880–1913', *Economic History Review*, 43: 329–55.

Feinstein, C.H., Matthews, R.C.O. and Odling-Smee, J. (1982), 'The

Timing of the Climacteric and Its Sectoral Incidence in the UK 1873–1913', in Kindleberger, C.P. and di Tella, G. (eds.), *Economics in the Long View: Essays in Honour of W.W. Rostow*, vol. III, Macmillan, London.

Feinstein, C.H. and Pollard, S. (eds.) (1988), *Studies in Capital Formation in the United Kingdom 1750–1920*, Oxford.

Floud, R. and McCloskey, D.N. (1994), *The Economic History of Britain Since 1700, Vol.II: 1860–1939*, Cambridge.

Foreman-Peck, J.S. (1979), 'Tariff Protection and Economies of Scale: The British Motor Car Industry Before 1939', *Oxford Economic Papers*, 31: 237–57.

(1981), 'The British Tariff and Industrial Protection in the 1930s: An Alternative Model', *Economic History Review*, 34: 132–9.

Fremdling, G. (1985), 'Did the US Transmit the Great Depression to the Rest of the World?', *American Economic Review*.

Friedman, M. and Schwartz, A.J. (1982), *Monetary Trends in the United States and in the United Kingdom, 1870–1970*, Chicago.

Friedman, P. (1978), 'An Econometric Model of National Income, Commercial Policy and the Level of International Trade: The Open Economies of Europe, 1924–1938', *Journal of Economic History*, 38: 148–80.

Galenson, W. and Zellner, A. (1957), 'International Comparison of Unemployment Rates', Universities-National Bureau Committee for Economic Research (ed.), *The Measurement and Behaviour of Unemployment*, Princeton University Press, Princeton.

Garside, W.R. and Hatton, T.J. (1985), 'Keynesian Policy and British Unemployment in the 1930s', *Economic History Review*, 38: 83–8.

Glickman, D.L. (1947), 'The British Imperial Preference System', *Quarterly Journal of Economics*, 61: 439–70.

Glynn, S. and Booth, A. (1983), 'Unemployment in Interwar Britain: A Case for Re-Learning the Lessons of the 1930s', *Economic History Review*, 36: 329–48.

Goldsmith, R.W. (1984), 'The Stability of the Ratio of Non Financial Debt to Income', *Banca Nazionale Del Lavoro Quarterly Review*, 150: 285–305.

Grassman, S. (1980), 'Long Term Trends in Openness of National Economies', *Oxford Economic Papers*, 32: 123–33.

Hatton, T.J. (1983), 'Unemployment Benefits and the Macroeconomics of the Inter-War Labour Market: a Further Analysis', *Oxford Economic Papers*, 35: 486–505.

(1984), 'Vacancies and Unemployment in the 1920s', Centre for Economic Policy Research Discussion Paper No.10.

(1985), 'The British Labor Market in the 1920s: A Test of the Search-Turnover Approach', *Explorations in Economic History*, 22: 257–70.

(1986), 'Structural Aspects of Unemployment in Britain Between the Wars', *Research in Economic History*, pp. 55–92.

(1988), 'A Quarterly Model of the Labour Market in Interwar Britain', *Oxford Bulletin of Economics and Statistics*, 50: 1–26.

(1988), 'The Recovery of the 1930s and Economic Policy in Britain', in Butlin, N. and Gregory, R.G. (eds.), *Recovery from the Depression: Australia and the World Economy in the 1930s*, Cambridge.

(1994), 'Unemployment and the Labour Market in Interwar Britain', in Floud, R. and McCloskey, D.N. (eds.), *The Economic History of Britain Since 1700, Vol.II: 1860–1939*, Cambridge.

Hicks, J.R. (1974), 'Real and Monetary Factors in Economic Fluctuations', *Scottish Journal of Political Economy*, 21, 3: 205–14.

(1982), 'Are There Economic Cycles', in Hicks, J.R. (ed.), *Money, Interest and Wages, Collected Essays on Economic Theory*, vol. II, Oxford.

Howson, S. (1974), 'The Origins of Dear Money, 1919–20', *Economic History Review*, 27: 88–107.

(1975), *Domestic Monetary Management in Britain 1919–38*, Cambridge University Press, Cambridge.

Humphries, J. (1987), 'Inter-war House Building, Cheap Money and Building Societies: The Housing Boom Revisited', *Business History*, 29, 3: 325–45.

Jones, M.E.F. (1985), 'The Regional Impact of an Overvalued Pound in the 1920s', *Economic History Review*, 38: 393–401.

Kahn, A.E. (1946), *Great Britain in the World Economy*, Sir Isaac Pitman, London.

Kaldor, N. (1977), 'The Nemesis of Free Trade', in Kaldor, N. (ed.), *Further Essays on Applied Economics*, Duckworth, London.

Kelvin, P. and Jarrett, J.E. (1985), *Unemployment: Its Social Psychological Effects*, Cambridge University Press, Cambridge.

Keynes, J.M. (1939), 'Relative Movements of Real Wages and Output',

185

Economic Journal, 49: 34–51.

(1925), *The Economic Consequences of Mr Churchill*, reprinted in *The Collected Writings of John Maynard Keynes*, vol. IX, 1972 (ed. D. Moggridge), St Martins Press, New York, pp.207–30.

Kindleberger, C.P. (1956), *The Terms of Trade: A European Case Study*, MIT, New York and London.

(1983), *The World in Depression, 1929–1939*, Harmondsworth.

Kitson, M. and Michie, J. (1994), 'Co-ordinated Deflation – The Tale of Two Recessions', in Michie, J. and Grieve Smith, J. (eds.), *Unemployment in Europe*.

Kitson, M. and Solomou, S.N. (1990), *Protectionism and Economic Revival: The British Interwar Economy*, Cambridge University Press, Cambridge.

(1991), 'Trade Policy and the Regionalization of Imports in Interwar Britain', *Bulletin of Economic Research*, 43, 2: 151–67.

Kitson, M., Solomou, S.N. and Weale, M.R. (1991), 'Effective Protection and Economic Recovery in the United Kingdom During the 1930s', *Economic History Review*, 44, 2: 328–38.

Kleinknecht, A. (1987), *Innovation Patterns in Crisis and Prosperity: Schumpeter's Long Cycle Reconsidered*, London.

Kondratieff, N.D. (1935), 'The Long Waves in Economic Life', *Review of Economic Statistics*, 17: 105–15.

Krugman, P. (1982), 'The Macroeconomics of Protection with a Floating Exchange Rate', *Carnegie-Rochester Conference Series on Public Policy*, 16: 141–82, North-Holland, Amsterdam.

(1984), 'Import protection as Export Promotion: International Competition in the Presence of Oligopoly and Economies of Scale', in Kierzkowski, H. (ed.), *Monopolistic Competition in International Trade*, Oxford University Press, Oxford.

(1987), 'Is Free Trade Passe?', *Economic Perspectives*, 1: 131–44.

Kydland, F.E. and Prescott, E.C. (1982), 'Time to Build and Aggregate Fluctuation', *Econometrica*, 50: 1345–70.

Leak, H. (1937), 'Some Results of the Import Duties Act', *Journal of the Royal Statistical Society*, 100, Part IV: 558–95.

Lebergott, S. (1964), *Manpower in Economic Growth*, McGraw-Hill, New York.

Lewis, W.A. (1952), 'World Production Prices and Trade 1870–1960', *The Manchester School*, 20: 105–38.

(1978), *Growth and Fluctuations 1870–1913*, Allen & Unwin, London.

Liepmann, H. (1938), *Tariff Levels and the Economic Unity of Europe*, Allen & Unwin, London.

Lindbeck, A. (1993): *Unemployment and Macroeconomics*, MIT Press, Cambridge, Mass.

Lomax, K.S. (1959), 'Production and Productivity Movements in the United Kingdom Since 1900', *Journal of the Royal Statistical Society*, Series A, 2: 185–220.

(1969), 'Growth and Productivity in the United Kingdom', in Aldcroft, D.H. and Fearon, P. (eds.), *Economic Growth in 20th-Century Britain*, Macmillan, London.

Lucas, R.E. (1981), *Studies in Business Cycle Theory*, Cambridge, Mass.

Lucas, R.E. Jr. (1987), *Models of Business Cycles*, Yrjo Jahnsson Lectures, Basil Blackwell/Oxford University Press, Oxford.

Maddison, A. (1964), *Economic Growth in the West*, Allen & Unwin, London.

(1982), *Phases of Capitalist Development*, Oxford University Press, Oxford.

(1991), *Dynamic Forces in Capitalist Development*, Oxford.

Maizels, A. (1963), *Industrial Growth and World Trade*, Cambridge, Cambridge University Press.

Malinvaud, E. (1978): *The Theory of Unemployment Reconsidered*, Basil Blackwell, Oxford.

Matthews, K.G.P. (1986), 'Was Sterling Overvalued in 1925?', *Economic History Review*, 39: 572–87.

Matthews, R.C.O, (1959), *The Trade Cycle*, Cambridge.

Matthews, R.C.O, Feinstein, C.H. and Odling-Smee, J.C. (1982), *British Economic Growth, 1856–1973*, Oxford University Press, Oxford.

McCloskey, D.N. (1970), 'Did Victorian Britain Fail?', *Economic History Review*, 23, 446–59.

(1974), 'Victorian Growth: A Rejoinder', *Economic History Review*, 27, 2: 275–7.

Middleton, R. (1981), 'The Constant Employment Budget Balance and British Budgetary Policy, 1929–39', *Economic History Review*, 34: 266–86.

Mills, T. (1991), 'Are Fluctuations in UK Output Transitory or Permanent?', *The Manchester School*, 59, 1: 1–11.

187

Mills, T. and Taylor, M.P. (1989), 'Random Walk Components in Output and Exchange Rates: Some Robust Tests on UK Data', *Bulletin of Economic Research*, 41, 2: 215–42.

Moggridge, D.E. (1972), *British Monetary Policy, 1924–31: The Norman Conquest of $4.86*, Cambridge University Press, Cambridge.

Morgan, E.V. (1952), *Studies in British Financial Policy, 1914–1925*, Macmillan, London.

Mundell, R.A. (1961), 'Flexible Exchange Rates and Employment Policy', *Canadian Journal of Economics*, 27: 509–17.

Nevin, E. (1955), *The Mechanism of Cheap Money*, University of Wales, Cardiff.

R. Nurkse (1944), *International Currency Experience*, League of Nations.

Pigou, A.C. (1927): 'Wage Policy and Unemployment', *Economic Journal*, 38: 355–68.

—— (1947), *Aspects of British Economic History, 1918–1925*, Frank Cass and Co. Ltd, London.

Pollard, S. (ed.), *The Gold Standard and Employment Policies Between the Wars*, Methuen, London.

Pressnell, L.S. (1978), '1925: The Burden of Sterling', *Economic History Review*, 31: 57–88.

Reddaway, W.B. (1970), 'Was $4.86 Inevitable in 1925?', *Lloyds Bank Review*, 96: 15–28.

Redmond, J. (1980), 'An Indicator of the Effective Exchange Rate of the Pound in the Nineteen-Thirties', *Economic History Review*, 33: 83–91.

—— (1984), 'The Sterling Overvaluation in 1925: A Multilateral Approach', *Economic History Review*, 37: 520–32.

—— (1988), 'Effective Exchange Rates in the Nineteen-Thirties: North America and the Gold Bloc', *Journal of European Economic History*, 17, 2: 379–410.

Richardson, H.W. (1967), *Economic Recovery in Britain, 1932–9*, Weidenfeld & Nicolson, London.

Robertson, A.J. (1983), 'British Rearmament and Industrial Growth, 1935–1939', *Research in Economic History*, 8: 279–309.

Rowthorn, R.E. and Solomou, S.N. (1991), 'The Macroeconomic Effects of Overseas Investment on the UK Balance of Trade, 1870-1913', *Economic History Review*, 44: 654–64.

Sayers, R.S.: 'The Return to Gold, 1925', in L.S. Pressnell (ed.), *Studies in the Industrial Revolution*, Athlone Press, University of London.

Sheffrin, S.M. (1988), 'Have Economic Fluctuations Been Dampened? A Look at Evidence Outside the United States', *Journal of Monetary Economics*, 21: 73–83.

Slutsky, E. (1937), 'The Summation of Random Causes as the Cause of Cyclical Processes', *Econometrica*, 5: 105–46.

Solomou, S.N. (1987), *Phases of Economic Growth, 1850–1973: Kondratieff Waves and Kuznets Swings*, Cambridge University Press, Cambridge.

— (1994), 'Economic Fluctuations, 1870–1913', in Floud, R. and McCloskey, D.N. (eds.).

Solomou, S.N. and Catao, L.A.V. (1994), 'Real Exchange Rates During the Classical Gold Standard 1870–1913: The Core Industrial Countries', Department of Applied Economics, Working Paper No. 9403, Cambridge University.

Solomou, S.N. and Weale, M.R. (1991), 'Balanced Estimates of UK GDP, 1870–1913', *Explorations in Economic History*, 28: 54–63.

— (1993), 'Balanced Estimates of National Accounts When Measurement Errors are Autocorrelated: The UK 1920–38', *Journal of the Royal Statistical Society*, series. A: 89–105.

— (1996), 'UK National Income 1920–1938', *Economic History Review*, February.

Svennilson, I. (1952), *Growth and Stagnation in the European Economy*, UNECE, Geneva.

Tarshis, L. (1939): 'Changes in Real and Money Wages', *Economic Journal*, 49, 1: 150–4.

Temin, P. (1989), *Lessons From the Great Depression*, Cambridge, Mass.

Thomas, B. (1973), *Migration and Economic Growth*, Cambridge.

Thomas, M. (1983), 'Rearmament and Economic Recovery in the Late 1930s', *Economic History Review*, 36: 559–79.

— (1994a), 'Wage Behaviour in Interwar Britain: A Sceptical Enquiry', in Grantham, G. and MacKinnon, M., *Labour Market Evolution: The Economic History of Market Integration, Wage Flexibility and the Employment Relation*, Routledge, London and New York.

— (1994b), 'The Macro-economics of the Interwar Years', in Floud, R. and McCloskey, D.N., (eds.) *The Economic History of Britain Since 1700*, vol. II.

Van Duijn, J.J. (1983), *The Long Wave in Economic Life*, Allen & Unwin, London.

Velupellai, N. and Thygesen, N. (eds.) (1990), *Business Cycles, Non*

Linearities, Disequilibria, and Simulations: Readings in Business Cycles Theory, London.

Von Tunzelmann, G.N. (1982), 'Structural Change and Leading Sectors in British Manufacturing 1907–68', in Kindleberger, C.P. and di Tella, G. (eds.), *Economics in the Long View: Essays in Honour of W.W. Rostow*, vol. III, Macmillan, London.

Worswick, G.D.N. (1984), 'Economic Recovery in the 1930s', *National Institute Economic Review*, 110: 85–93.

Wright, J.F. (1981), 'Britain's Interwar Experience', in Eltis, W.A. and Sinclair, P.J.N. (eds.), *The Money Supply and Exchange Rate*, Oxford University Press, Oxford.

Youngson, A.J. (1960), *The British Economy 1920–1957*, Allen & Unwin, London.

INDEX OF NAMES

191

INDEX OF NAMES

Keynes, J.M.   34, 36, 72, 79
Kindleberger, C.P.   101
Kitson, M.   47, 126, 133, 142, 145, 146, 147, 153, 154, 157, 160
Kleinknecht, A.   2
Kochin, L.A.   5, 64–6, 112
Kondratieff, N.D.   1

Leak, H.   143–5
Liepmann, H.   132, 133
Lindbeck, A.   81
Lucas, R.E.   106–8, 111

McKenna, R.   132
Maddison, A.   2–5, 54, 116, 117, 118, 120
Maizels, A.   145
Malinvaud, E.   57
Matthews, K.P.   38, 79
Matthews, R.C.O.   2, 70, 88, 153, 178
Middleton, R.   97
Mills, T.C.   12, 104
Moggridge, D.E.   24, 41, 42, 122
Mundell, R.A.   137, 157

Nickell, S.   72, 74
Nurkse, R.   159

Pigou, A.C.   5, 56, 82

Redmond, J.   36, 37, 121, 145
Richardson, H.   125, 147–50
Rowthorn, R.E.   103

Sachs, J.   112, 116, 120–1, 127
Scheffrin, S.M.   88
Schumpeter, J.A.   99
Slutsky, E.   89
Solomou, S.N.   2, 6, 38, 47, 85, 88, 94–5, 103, 104, 105, 126, 133, 142, 145, 146, 147, 153, 154, 157, 160
Summers, L.   66

Tarshis, L.   72
Temin, P.   4, 102, 160
Thomas, B.   103
Thomas, M.   68, 77

Van Duijn, J.J.   2

Warburton, P.   64, 72, 74, 79
Warswick, G.D.N.   72, 74, 126
Weale, M.   6, 85, 94–5, 105
Webber, A.   96
Wood, G.   96

Zellner, A.   54

INDEX OF SUBJECTS

193

195